THE SACRED ART of RUSSIA
FROM IVAN THE TERRIBLE TO PETER THE GREAT

FROM THE STATE HISTORICAL MUSEUM, MOSCOW

GEORGIA INTERNATIONAL CULTURAL EXCHANGE, INC.

This publication is the catalogue for the exhibition
*The Sacred Art of Russia from Ivan the Terrible
to Peter the Great*, held at the Cobb Galleria Centre,
Atlanta, May 13 through July 25, 1995.

Published by the Georgia International Cultural Exchange, Inc.,
Atlanta, Georgia

Editors: Paula Marlais Hancock, Carolyn S. Vigtel, Margaret Wallace
Editorial consultant: Maria Lunk
Editorial assistant: Laura Brannan

Design: Times 3, Atlanta
Map: Ann Fowler, Atlanta
Printing: Geographics, Atlanta

Photo Credits
State Historical Museum, Moscow: V. M. Bojko,
M. N. Kravtsov, V. A. Mochugovsky, V. P. Roden;
Atlanta: Steve Carmichael, pages 19, 20, 21, 23

Front cover: MITER, 1685, cat. no. 337.
Back cover: ICON OF THE DESCENT INTO HELL (ANASTASIS),
mid-16th century, cat. no. 27.

Library of Congress No. 95-076285
ISBN 09646394-0-8 (soft bound)
ISBN 09646394-1-6 (hard bound)

CONTENTS

SPONSORS

PREFACE

CHARLES P. GRAHAM
Executive Director, Georgia International
Cultural Exchange, Inc., and
Lieutenant General, U. S. Army Retired

During the past half-century, we in the West have lacked a true understanding of Russia and its people due to the adversarial relationship existing between our two countries. This has been most unfortunate since Russian history is a captivating story–full of struggle, mystery and romance. Russia has a fascinating culture that has been developed, molded, altered, and then remolded again and again as people of many origins exerted their influences in the crucible that is Russia. Into the vast Russian melting pot came the Scythians, Byzantines, Tartars, Swedes, Poles, Lithuanians, and many others–each adding their particular ingredient to what was then Russia. Yet throughout the centuries, the strong, determined, yet fun-loving, approach to life inherent in the native Russians who were born into the vast reaches of wild land and demanding environment always dominated in this potpourri of life. Throughout all this change, one institution remained solid–the Orthodox Church and its intimate role in the lives of the Russian people.

To the tsars, the royal courtesans, the merchants, the peasants, and especially the serfs, the Church provided hope--hope for tomorrow, the day after tomorrow, and forever. Beginning with the late tenth century when Prince Vladimir of Kiev made Christianity the state religion, the people looked to the Church and its liturgy to help them survive the struggle of a life burdened by an autocratic political system from which none could flee, a social structure that offered limited hope for a better life, and a land and climate that challenged the most hearty. Religious icons became a source of spiritual strength for all the people wherever they were: in their homes, at their labors in the field or shop, traveling throughout their vast land, on the seemingly endless battlefields, and naturally in their beautiful onion-domed churches and cathedrals.

Their religion relied on art to tell the spiritual story of Christianity from the beginning through its spread by devoted disciples to the far corners of their native land. These sacred art objects greeted them when they arose each day to face their struggle of survival. Their religion and its icons gave them strength to defend their land and lives from the many invaders who came to conquer and destroy their unique way of life. It provided inspiration to those who were the cultural pioneers in the arts—story, song, verse, dance, and drama. It encouraged the architects, the builders, the inventors, the merchants, the financiers, the farmers, and all who strove to learn and make a better life for all. Even after seventy years of Communist rule and the state's determined efforts to wipe out religion, the faith of the Russian people and their traditional art have survived. This is the story that *The Sacred Art of Russia from Ivan the Terrible to Peter the Great* tells—the story of a people and their lives as seen through their art. It is a story worth telling over and over, for it is unique in the annals of history.

As a reader, you may wonder why Ivan the Terrible and Peter the Great were included in our exhibition title when, in fact, many of the objects precede and follow these tsars by centuries. Since the early days of the Church in Kiev, Russian artists continually toiled to perfect the technique of icon painting until, during the reign of Ivan the Terrible in the sixteenth century, it reached its zenith. Then, around 1700, during the reign of Peter the Great, the hint of decline in ancient Russian traditions was accelerated by Peter's forcible changes in the culture of Russia. Particularly noticeable was the shift away from the required stylistic painting of icons. Thus, these autocratic rulers played central roles in this story of Russian art, the first as a champion, the second as a force of redirection.

There are many to whom we are deeply indebted for enabling us to tell this story. First is Dr. Alexander Shkurko, the General Director of the State Historical Museum in Moscow, who was willing to work closely with an unknown group of Georgians to produce this magnificent exhibition. We are most grateful to him for having faith in us. Second are the State Historical Museum's most capable assistants and talented staff of curators who have worked diligently to prepare the many pieces of beautiful art for their trip to the United States and have trusted their priceless possessions to our care. They provided the essays that set the stage for understanding how these beautiful objects of art affected the Russian people and valuable information about each piece. Without them, the exhibition would have been only a dream. For the fortitude to make that dream a reality, we will always be indebted to Mark A. Johnson, Esq., and Commissioner Gordon J. Wysong of Cobb County, Georgia. They persevered over many obstacles to ensure their dream came true.

This exhibition project is, by any definition, out of the ordinary and to have accomplished it in less than a year was an extraordinary challenge to the those involved. Just displaying this collection of beautiful art required a setting that reflected a keen understanding of the art, the religion whose story it told, and the people whose lives were involved. We were most fortunate to have the installation developed by the noted Russian designer Alexander Mironov, who had been named Distinguished Artist of Russia in 1981. With the glittering brilliance of the objects, the environment created by Mr. Mironov conveys the unmistakable feeling of awe and mystery so pronounced in Russian church art.

Others involved deserve special recognition. There were the citizens and businesses of Cobb County and the greater Atlanta area who, when asked, stepped forward cheerfully and enthusiastically, knowing they had an opportunity to be a part of a unique cultural experience. Then there were the many volunteers whose warm smile and dedicated talents assisted you, our visitors, in enjoying the exhibition. Each of them cheerfully gave many hours to undergo training and serve as a volunteer. The success of the exhibition owes much to all of them.

Most important were the dedicated professionals who came together from many varying walks of life to form the staff—a close-knit team that, although handicapped by limited time and often even more limited funds, made this exhibition a truly magnificent event. Amongst this fine group, one merits special recognition—Gudmund Vigtel, who has served as Director of Cultural and Educational Activities. He brought to the team many years of experience and love for fine art, twenty-eight of which he served as Director of the High Museum of Art here in Atlanta. Vig's tremendous knowledge and expertise have skillfully guided us through what has been a real learning exprerience that has culminated in this truly extrordinary exhibition. To Vig and each member of the team, I owe my sincere thanks and will cherish our association forever. Finally, to my wife Alice who has had limitless patience through these past ten months, I give my eternal gratitude.

RUSSIAN AND AMERICAN COMMITTEES

RUSSIAN COMMITTEE OF HONOR

Eugeny Y. Sidorov
The Minister of Culture

Yuli M. Vorontsov
The Ambassador of the Russian
Federation to the United States

Juvenaly
The Metropolitan of Krutitsy and
Kolomna

Alexander I. Shkurko
Director of the State Historical Museum

THE ORGANIZING COMMITTEE

Tamara G. Igumnova
Vice Director of the State Historical
Museum

Tatjana T. Ivanova
Vice Director of the State Historical
Museum

Tatjana I. Sizova
Chief Curator of the State Historical
Museum

Guenrikh P. Popov
Art Historian

Anatoly I. Venedukhine
Historian

Andrey L. Anikeev
Art Critic

Conservators of the
State Historical Museum:
A. G. Ryabenkov, P. M. Sheparev,
N. N. Voronov, F. E. Prendel,
L. A. Kologrevova, M. A. Kuznetsova,
I. E. Gogoleva, O. N. Sotskova,
N. A. Chastlevaia, U. V. Matveeva,
A. D. Marchenkova, A. N. Hetagurov

Computer Support:
K. E. Poluektov
K. A. Meerov

FOREWORD

ALEXANDER SHKURKO
General Director
State Historical Museum, Moscow

The State Historical Museum is pleased to introduce one of its most important collections to the American public. Established in 1872, the State Historical Museum is located in Red Square in the heart of Moscow. Several generations of scholars, collectors, and curators were responsible for forming its extensive collections, and, today, the Museum has 4.5 million art objects and 12 million document pages, which reflect the historical and cultural heritage of Russia.

From Eurasian nomadic arts and crafts of the first millennium B.C., to medieval icons, to the Russian avant garde, the Museum's collections reveal Russia's artistic contribution to world culture. The works in this exhibition represent a part of this contribution and remarkable heritage.

Icons, church vessels, vestments, and jewelry have more than functional links with religion. They reflect the artistic philosophy of their anonymous makers and the Orthodox Christian concept of humankind's mission in a world ruled by divine powers.

Christian unity as the pillar of society, Christian piety as the basic moral norm, ascetic resignation as the way to salvation– these principles seemed to leave little room for the artist's aesthetic self-expression, for historical or everyday realities, or for personal likes and dislikes. But in this atmosphere of inviolable aesthetic and philosophical standards for the arts, surviving intact for centuries in monastic seclusion, sublime works were created. The works of Andrei Rublev and Dionysius, for example, reached incomparable heights. Their icons and murals suggested the idea of perfection, unity, and eternity as divine creation imbued with light.

The canons of Orthodox Christianity filled icons with symbolism. Yet, in cities and powerful princedoms across Russia, neither these conventions nor the old traditions of Russian art closed artists' hearts to the atmosphere of their time. Political and social forces were powerless to change the basic patterns and aesthetic principles of art, but they determined the milieu in which works appeared and existed. Art obliquely reflected the tastes and opinions of church hierarchy and feudal rulers, and at the same time, in closed medieval communities, the style of particular artists or schools began to develop and be expressed. Their powerful, expressive imagery produced dramatic and beautiful pictures and unforgettable color.

Today, this vast cultural panorama exists only in fragments. Fires, military invasions, and neglect have meant the loss of some of Russia's cultural heritage. Therefore, it is the responsibility of the Museum to protect and preserve art and artifacts for the coming generations.

The future of a global civilization depends largely on understanding cultural traditions and recognizing their value. With this in mind, the State Historical Museum gladly accepted the invitation of the Georgia International Cultural Exchange, supported by the Cobb County Board and the Governor of the State of Georgia, to participate in the exhibition *The Sacred Art of Russia from Ivan the Terrible to Peter the Great.* We hope this exhibition will honorably contribute to the cultural program of the 1996 Olympics in Atlanta. ❖

MAP

The dark outlines on the map indicate the provinces established by Tsar Peter I (Peter the Great).

Each province was administered by a governor who reported to the tsar.

A. V. LAVRENTIEV

THE RUSSIAN STATE AND CHURCH: TWELVE CENTURIES OF HISTORY

It is difficult to select a specific event or date to begin the narrative of Russian history. The legendary dates of the founding of Kiev, the capital of Old Russia, in A.D. 482 and the arrival from Scandinavia in A.D. 852 of Rurik, the founder of the ruling dynasty, are key events, but the principal date in Russian history was probably the year A.D. 988 when the great Prince Vladimir I Christianized Russia in accordance with the Orthodox rite of the Byzantine Church.

From the ninth through the first half of the eleventh century, the vast territories inhabited by Eastern Slavs were united into one state with the Baltic Sea in the north, the Black Sea in the south, the Carpathian mountains in the west, and the great forests beyond the Volga River in the east. Kiev became the capital and here ruled the dynasty of grand princes descended from Rurik. Two of them, Vladimir (ruled 980–1015), the saint who Christianized Russia, and his son Jaroslav the Wise (r. 1015–45), influenced not only Russia's history but also her cultural growth. Under their reign, churches were erected and decorated with frescoes, mosaics, icons, and precious religious objects. This brought architects, painters, and artisans to Russia from the entire Orthodox world. It was also at this time that Russia's first schools were opened.

The richness of the Russian Orthodox ritual–its splendor and refinement–was to a large degree the contribution of artists. But beyond the churches, artists had regular patrons in the Russian people. Icons and Gospels could be found in the home of every Orthodox Christian, be it a palace or a peasant's hut. Crosses or small icons were also worn by most people. Pious Christians of all social strata made donations to monasteries and churches of everything from jeweled masterpieces to crude objects by rural woodcarvers. Traditions of religious art were forming in Russia, developing a strong history inseparable from the history of the state.

After the death of St. Vladimir, Russia suffered from power struggles among his descendants. This period of feudal warfare, which lasted for two centuries, eventually produced more than ten separate principalities, with Kiev at the center of continuous fighting. But despite the volatile political climate, significant cultural development took place during this early period of Russian history, particularly in the new capitals of the independent states. The fortified cities of Novgorod and Pskov in the northwest and Vladimir and Rostov in the northeast emerged as centers of urban culture, along with more than four hundred smaller towns. Among these small towns was Moscow, mentioned for the first time in the chronicles in 1147, and built as a border fortress for one of the Rostov-Suzdal principalities.

In religion, however, Russia remained united, and the Orthodox clergy made great efforts to reconcile the warring princes. The head of the Russian Orthodox Church, the Metropolitan of Kiev, enjoyed enormous power and authority, since his church was territorially the largest in the Orthodox world. Formally the Russian Orthodox Church was one of sixty churches under the Patriarch of Constantinople, but in many respects, it occupied a special position. In fact, two native Russians were appointed metropolitans in the eleventh and twelfth centuries, despite the custom of appointing metropolitans from Constantinople. By the end of the sixteenth century, the Russian Church had become almost completely independent, with its own patriarchate.

Russia suffered a major catastrophe in 1237 when the Mongols invaded from the southeast under the command of Batu Khan, the nephew of Genghis Khan. The Russians offered heroic resistance, but over the next three years of devastating raids, thousands were killed, and Russia was destroyed. The Mongols created a nomadic state in Russia, which they called the Golden Horde, putting an end to the first period of Russian national history.

Russian culture suffered significant damage as a result of Mongol domination. The destruction of the cities and towns meant that centers of art and learning were lost, as well as the art objects. By the time of the Mongol invasions, thousands of churches had been built in Russia and filled with icons, but today, only slightly more than thirty icons from the pre-Mongolian period survive. The loss of the artists, killed or enslaved in the fighting, and the huge tributary payments demanded by the Golden Horde, which cut deeply into the treasuries of the churches and the estates of the Russian princes, left few resources for Russia's cultural renewal.

National revival meant enormous labor and sacrifice. Towns were slowly rebuilt, industry and trade resumed, abandoned fields were plowed. Success, however, came only after some degree of unification among the Russian principalities. The Mongol invasion had demonstrated the cost of squabbling and separatism by the princes of Russia.

At the beginning of the fourteenth century, the princes of Moscow began to lead the movement toward a unified Russia. Grand Duke Ivan Kalita (r. 1325–40), the second of Rurik's descendants to rule Moscow and an outstanding politician, was the founder of the dynasty of Moscow princes and Russian tsars, who ruled until the end of the sixteenth century. The success of

Ivan Kalita and his descendants could already be seen by 1380 when the Golden Horde suffered their first defeat at the hands of the united armies of the Russian princes, led by Kalita's grandson, Dimitri Donskoy of Moscow.

During this period, the Russian Orthodox Church supported the Moscow princes. In the fourteenth century, the metropolitan of the Church moved permanently to Moscow, and in the fifteenth century, the residence of the metropolitan symbolically neighbored the newly-built grand princely palace in the Kremlin.

The liberation and unification of Russian lands around Moscow was completed by the end of the fifteenth century under Ivan III (also known as Ivan the Great, r. 1462–1505), who declared himself Sovereign of All Russia. The Principality of Moscow, using the double-headed eagle as its coat of arms, began to play a significant role in international politics.

The sixteenth and seventeenth centuries were a time of further expanding and strengthening Russia. Diplomatic ties stretched as far as London and Madrid in the west and Beijing and Delhi in the east, and the annexation of the vast territories of Siberia moved Russia's borders up to China and Pacific Ocean.

The internal affairs of Russia at this time were complex. Ivan IV (r. 1533–84), the first of the princes to crown himself tsar, ruled during a period of exhausting territorial wars and the bloody repressions of real and imagined enemies, which won him the nickname Ivan the Terrible. When his son Fedor I (r. 1584–98) died without an heir, there followed a period of crisis, known as the Time of Troubles. Savage battling over succession to the throne, as well as foreign military invasion, placed the country on the brink of catastrophe.

In 1613, after the defeat of many internal and external enemies, seventeen-year-old Michael Romanov was elected tsar, beginning a dynasty that ruled Russia until 1917.

The history of the Russian Orthodox Church is inseparable from that of the country during this period. Church leaders were often involved in the politics of their day, and some were even executed for political reasons. Metropolitan Philip, a martyr who objected to the tyranny of Ivan the Terrible, and Patriarch Germogen, who gave his life resisting foreign invaders, were both canonized in the seventeenth century.

The establishment of a patriarchate in Russia in 1589 was the most important landmark in Russian Orthodoxy. It marked the separation of the Russian Orthodox Church from the jurisdiction of the Eastern Orthodox Church in Constantinople and demonstrated the importance of the Russian state. The Russian

Patriarchs of the sixteenth and seventeenth centuries served as protectors of the first printing houses in Russia and the first school of higher education, founded in Moscow in 1686. As in earlier times, the Church was among the chief patrons of artists, architects, goldsmiths, jewelers, and woodcarvers.

The fourth of the Romanov tsars, Peter the Great (r. 1682–1725), pledged to modernize and Westernize Russia. He established many reforms and innovations, from bringing heavy industry to Russia to forcing Russians to adopt European-style clothing and shave their beards. Driven by inexhaustible energy, Peter spared no effort to achieve his goals, and set an example by working himself on many different projects. Cities and roads were built; the military was modernized; administrative reforms were instituted, including the creation of the Russian Senate; the Academy of Sciences was founded; and European scientists, scholars, craftsmen, and artists were encouraged to come to Russia.

Within a few decades, Russia had been turned into a full-fledged European power. In 1703, as a symbol of this new era of Russian history, Peter founded the city of St. Petersburg, declaring it the capital of Russia and the "window to Europe." In 1721, to mark his victory over Sweden for access to the Baltic Sea, Peter had himself declared Emperor of Russia.

The reforms that consolidated the tsar's power did not spare the Russian Orthodox Church. After the death of the tenth Russian Patriarch in 1700, patriarchal elections ceased, and ten years later, the Sacred Synod, a state body run by a bureaucrat, was entrusted with the administration of the Church. Further Church reforms were carried out by Peter's successors, particularly in the late eighteenth century by Catherine the Great.

Peter the Great died in 1725 without choosing a successor, which led to several decades of palace intrigue and coups by various factions. While the rule of Empress Elizabeth (r. 1741–61) was notable for its successes, it was the reign of Catherine II, known as Catherine the Great (r. 1762–96), that brought real stability and reforms to Russia. Catherine had been born Princess Sophia of Anhalt-Zerbst, and she was married to the future Peter III in 1744. When Peter's political enemies deposed and then killed him, Catherine, who was popular among the powerful nobility, was proclaimed ruler. An author herself, Catherine was a great patron of the arts, and her reign became synonymous with the Russian Age of Enlightenment.

The eighteenth century brought great changes to Russian art and culture. Westernization of Russian court life, the result of reforms by Peter the Great, changed the tastes and habits of

Russian nobility. In fact, a Russian nobleman of the Age of Enlightenment looked very little like his great-grandfather, but a great deal like his European contemporaries. However, among the lower classes of Russia—both rural and urban—Westernization was not embraced as whole-heartedly. This meant that the art and architecture created during this century became an interesting mix of traditional Russian and new European influences.

It was during the reign of Catherine the Great's grandson Alexander I (r. 1801–25) that Russia faced the Napoleonic Wars. Bloody clashes on European battlefields, Napoleon's invasion in 1812, the seizure and burning of Moscow, the heroic resistance of the Russian people, and finally Napoleon's inglorious retreat culminated in a victorious march by Russian regiments through Paris in 1814.

Patriotic enthusiasm drew the attention of many educated liberal Russians to the serious internal problems of the country. Most of the population remained, as they had for centuries, without rights or power—serfs bound to landowners. The nineteenth century was marked by a quest for a solution to this problem.

Pressed by growing discontent, Alexander II (r. 1855–81) instituted reforms to free the serfs, but ultimately, without the creation of a parliament or a constitution, his reforms were seen as insufficient by many of the more radical populist groups in Russia. Attempts to suppress this political opposition, eventually led to Alexander II's assassination. Further repression of the political left, as well as the persecution of minorities, by Alexander III (r. 1881–94) and Nicholas II (r. 1894–1917) finally erupted in the bloody revolutions of the early twentieth century and the execution of Nicholas and his family.

At this same time, Russian culture was going through a brilliant era. The nineteenth and early twentieth century gave the world Tolstoy, Dostoyevsky, Glinka, Moussorgsky, Diaghilev, Chaliapin, and many other writers, scientists, poets, and statesmen.

The Russian Orthodox Church was integral to this cultural movement. The exploration of religious and philosophical ideas and a renewed interest in the country's past and sources of national identity meant that artists, architects, and composers, of this so-called Silver Age found their inspiration in the Orthodox artistic tradition. It is because of this tradition that the Russian modernist movement had its unique national features, realized in the best works of the masters of the late nineteenth and early twentieth centuries. ✤

THE NOVODEVICHY CONVENT

I. G. BORISENKO

The Novodevichy, or New Maiden's, Convent in Moscow (fig. 1) is a remarkable architectural ensemble and the backdrop for many dramatic episodes in Russian history. Over five centuries, masters of different periods contributed to the creation of the buildings in this complex, which include the Mother of God of Smolensk Cathedral (Smolensk Cathedral), small churches, palace chambers, modest nuns' quarters, fortress walls, watch towers, a hospital, and a bell tower.

In 1922, the government turned Novodevichy into a museum, and since 1934, it has been a branch of the State Historical Museum, displaying a major collection of Russian icons and decorative arts objects. Restorations in recent years have attempted to return much of this important monument to its original appearance.

The Convent was founded in 1524 by Grand Duke Vasily III (ruled 1505–33), who built it to mark his victory over Lithuania in a battle for the ancient city of Smolensk. Vasily donated three thousand rubles in silver and villages owned by his Court to the Novodevichy Convent to help establish its economy. Vasily's son, Ivan the Terrible, the first tsar of Russia (born 1530, inherited the principality of Moscow in 1533, proclaimed himself tsar in 1547, died 1584), supported the Convent with significant gifts and had his daughter Anna baptized there. Later, Ivan sent relatives to the Convent, including former wives, as well as widows of noblemen and women of nobility who had fallen into disgrace and were forced to take the veil.

In 1598, Irina Godunova, widow of Tsar Fedor I (r. 1584–98) entered the Novodevichy Convent, and her brother Boris Godunov, who was then Regent of Russia, lived at the Convent briefly until, with the support of the Russian Patriarch, he was elected tsar. With lavish donations from Tsar Boris Godunov, the Smolensk Cathedral was renovated and the old wooden fence was replaced by stone walls. These new fortress walls protected the noble residents and also allowed the Convent to be used as a military outpost, with a garrison of Streltsy (soldiers of the Russian army), to protect against Tatar raids from the south.

During the Time of Troubles, a lawless period in the early years of the seventeenth century, the Convent was badly damaged in battles between the Russian militia and Polish and Lithuanian forces. An account written during this time tells that forces came to the suburbs of Moscow, captured the Novodevichy Convent, took the nuns to camps, and burned the Convent. A decisive battle in 1612, which took place near the Convent walls, liberated Moscow from the Polish invaders.

The Convent reached the height of its prosperity toward the end of the seventeenth century while Peter the Great's older half-sister Sophia was Regent (r. 1682–89). Her lavish donations to the Convent were probably made with the intention of creating a comfortable refuge for herself and female relatives.

When her younger brother Peter came of age in 1689, Sophia was unwilling to give up her power, and she conspired with the Kremlin Streltsy to keep control of the government. Peter organized his own forces and defeated his sister, banishing her to the Novodevichy Convent. Nine years later, after another failed attempt to regain power, Sophia was forced to take the veil and retire permanently to the Convent. In October of 1698, public executions of the traitorous Streltsy took place all over Moscow. One hundred and ninety-three of them were taken to the Convent and hanged outside of Sophia's windows. She died in 1704 and was buried in the Smolensk Cathedral. Novodevichy Convent fell into a period of neglect during the reign of Peter the Great, who had little use for the Church and its clergy. He imposed a tax on the Church, including the convents, and placed them under the administration of a government bureaucracy. In the 1720s, an orphanage was built in the Convent and a military hospital was housed there.

FIG. 1
The Novodevichy Convent

By the middle of the eighteenth century, however, Novodevichy had become one of the wealthiest convents in Russia—second only to the Ascension Convent in the Kremlin. Over fifteen thousand serfs were under the Convent's control, as well as thousands of acres of land and thirty-six villages. This land, as well as property within the city limits of Moscow, meant substantial administrative responsibilities for the Convent. A steward and a staff were employed to collect taxes, regulate relations with neighboring landowners, and sort out peasant complaints.

During Napoleon's occupation of Moscow in 1812, French troops seized the Convent. Most of the nuns fled, and the French used the Convent as a fortified warehouse. When they withdrew from Moscow, Napoleon gave the order to blow up the Smolensk Cathedral, the Refectory, the nuns' living quarters, and the Church of the Assumption. The nuns who had stayed behind, however, managed to extinguish the fuses on the barrels of gunpowder, and Novodevichy Convent was saved.

FIG. 2
The Mother of God
of Smolensk Cathedral

Except for a period from the end of the eighteenth century until 1868 when the Convent was used in part as a reformatory for women convicted by the Church Court, life at the Convent continued unchanged and without other major incidents until its closure in 1922.

Novodevichy Convent was built at an important crossroads between major land and water routes–the Smolensk Road and the Moscow River. The main buildings were positioned on intersecting north–south and east–west axes with the Mother of God of Smolensk Cathedral in the center. By the end of the seventeenth century, the area within the Convent walls had divided into a northern official half and a southern half with service buildings. The northern half included the Cathedral Square, a courtyard formed between the Cathedral, the gates, and two facing buildings containing nuns' quarters.

During the early years, only the Smolensk Cathedral was built of stone. Over time, the other wooden structures were replaced by bricks and white limestone, although some of the service and residential buildings were still made of wood well into the nineteenth century. The Smolensk Cathedral (fig. 2), constructed from 1524 to 1525, has five domes and a spacious interior. It has an aisle only on the eastern side, although excavations have revealed that there was once another aisle on the west. A wide ambulatory surrounds the Cathedral on four sides. While it was built as the main church of the Convent, it was used only during the warmer months of spring, summer, and fall. (Even modern attempts to adequately heat the Cathedral have failed.)

The Church of St. Ambrose, the Refectory, and the private residence of Irina Godunova were built next to the Cathedral. For a while, the Church of St. Ambrose was used as the Convent church during the winter. Later it was adopted as part of the hospital facilities and connected to the Church of the Assumption (fig. 3) by a covered passageway.

Novodevichy Convent covers an area of over twelve acres. The fortress walls, reaching thirty-five feet in places, add up to more than a half a mile in circumference and are fortified with twelve towers. In their current form, the walls bear a strong resemblance to the walls of the Kremlin. Several stone structures were built partially into the walls and apparently at one time served as living quarters for Sophia and Peter the Great's other sisters.

New construction at the end of the seventeenth century took older architectural styles into account while introducing new decorative elements. Six stone buildings were added to the com-

20

plex during this period, including a spacious Refectory and a five-tiered, 230-foot bell tower. A disastrous fire in 1796 badly damaged the Convent, and subsequent restoration has altered the original appearance of some of these buildings.

The Smolensk Cathedral has preserved the main features of Russian churches, with its frescoes and iconostasis. Built by Vasily III to commemorate his military victory, some of the Cathedral decorations suggest his particular interests. Along with Christian themes, scenes from Russian history decorate the walls. Among the saints depicted are Russian princes who had been canonized and images of saint-empresses of the Byzantine Empire, since Vasily's mother was one of the last Byzantine princesses.

The main theme of the Cathedral frescoes is the Acathistus, the solemn mass sung in honor of the Mother of God. It is divided into three parts, telling the events of the life of the Virgin, offering praise, and presenting the tenets of faith. The central image in the Cathedral is the icon *The Mother of God Hodegitria*, which is located in the lunette of the triumphal arch.

Novodevichy Convent was particularly privileged by its close connection to Moscow's princes. Many of the icons and other religious objects in its collection were produced as royal commissions at the Armory Chamber (state supported artists' workshops) of the Kremlin. Donations were made not only for the churches of the Convent, but also for the cells of tsaritsas and tsarevnas, the wives and daughters of tsars, who lived there as nuns.

The large iconostasis in the Smolensk Cathedral (partly on view in this exhibition) was particularly important among these royal donations. In the Local, or lower tier, are icons donated by the Russian tsars, from Ivan the Terrible to Peter the Great. One of the oldest icons in the iconostasis, *The Mother of God* (cat. no. 40) in the Deesis tier, is a copy of an icon in the Cathedral of the Annunciation in the Moscow Kremlin.

Boris Godunov donated the colorful icon of the martyrs Boris and Gleb (cat. no. 35), and he also ordered icons for the Deesis and the Festival, Prophets, and Forefathers tiers, as well as the panels of the second and third rows. The carved and gilt frame of the iconostasis was made between 1683 and 1685, during the period when Sophia was Regent of Russia. Originally the iconostasis reached the Cathedral's vault, but during restoration in the twentieth century, the uppermost tier was taken down.

Besides the icons of the iconostasis, the Convent's collection includes two thousand additional images. Noteworthy is the "measurement" icon, painted in 1650 for Sophia's sister Evdokiia

FIG. 3
*The Church of
the Assumption*

21

with the image of St. Evdokiia (cat. no. 78). Icons like this were painted for all the children of Tsar Alexis–the length of the icon corresponding to the size of the newly born child.

The work of metalsmiths and jewelers is also well represented in the collections. A silver basin for holy water was donated by Ivan the Terrible in 1581 (cat. no. 168, fig. 4), and many other objects came to the Convent from the Tsar's family.

Embroidery was the artistic contribution of Russian women during these centuries, and the beautiful work created by the nuns of the Convent workshops greatly enriched Novodevichy's collections. The nuns produced church vestments of rich import-ed or domestic textiles, often adorned with pearls and precious stones. The traditions of the convent workshops were continued into the beginning of the twentieth century, but by that time, the materials were less elaborate and costly. This change can be seen in the vestments and saccos made after designs by V. M. Vasnetsov (cat. no. 317, fig. 5).

While the collections of the Novodevichy Convent came pri-marily from gifts, the Convent workshops contributed to the collections as well. Today, these paintings and decorative objects make up the most significant part of the treasures of the State Historical Museum. ❖

FIG. 4
Basin for Holy Water

FIG. 5
Robe

THE CATHEDRAL OF THE INTERCESSION

A. S. USPENSKAIA

FIG. 1

*The Cathedral of
the Intercession*

The jewel of Russian architecture is the Cathedral of the Intercession (fig. 1), also known as St. Basil's, in Moscow. Commissioned by Tsar Ivan the Terrible and Metropolitan Macarius, the Cathedral was built to commemorate the 1552 victory over the Tatars of Kazan, descendants of the Mongol Golden Horde. The Cathedral was designed by Russian architects Postnik and Barma and constructed near the walls of the Kremlin from 1555 to 1561.

The tsar and the Russian people believed that the victory over the Tatars had been accomplished through the intercession of the Mother of God, who had spread her *Pokrov* (protective veil) over the Russian soldiers. For this reason, the central portion of the Cathedral was consecrated in honor of the Feast of Pokrov, or the Feast of the Intercession.

The Cathedral is an unusual ensemble of nine chapels, with the 152-foot Pokrov Chapel towering over the rest. In contrast to the eight other domed chapels, the Pokrov Chapel is topped by a high-peaked tower with a golden onion-shaped cupola. The chapels are connected with galleries, creating a kind of visual and spiritual unity.

In 1588, the small Chapel of St. Basil was added, named for the "Holy Fool" who had renounced the world and devoted himself to the service of God, denouncing even Ivan the Terrible for his misdeeds. Basil was buried under the Cathedral of the Intercession, and gradually, his name became the popular designation for the building.

The Cathedral was not intended for year-round services, since it was never heated. The interior spaces are not large, the biggest being only about 500 square feet. Fire and renovations have wrought many changes in the building. The earliest depiction of the Cathedral is an engraving in a book entitled *Journey to Moscovia* by Adam Olearius (cat. no. 363), published in the early seventeenth century. A twentieth-century model of the Cathedral (cat. no. 372, fig. 2) shows the subsequent changes made to the building. After a fire in 1593, the cupolas were changed to the onion shape, and the vivid colors were added in the 1840s. The Cathedral of the Intercession was turned into the Museum of Architecture in 1923; five years later it became a branch of the State Historical Museum.

Based on scholarly research, the Cathedral has been restored to the way it looked in the seventeenth and eighteenth centuries. The painting on the facade, which imitates masonry, the white stone, the multicolored cupolas, the golden spirals, and the decorative tiles make this a vivid and striking monument.

FIG. 2
*Model of the Cathedral
of the Intercession*

On the interior, areas of restoration have included the painted imitation masonry in the Pokrov Chapel, from the time of Ivan the Terrible, and the floral painting and images of saints from the eighteenth century. Restorers also uncovered a decorative fresco under many layers of paint and an inscription in the eaves giving the date of completion of the Cathedral as June 29, 1561.

Icons from the Cathedral's collections include *The Intercession of the Mother of God* (cat. no. 102, fig. 3), from the late seventeenth or early eighteenth century, which depicts the miraculous appearance of the Mother of God in Constantinople. Against the background of the church, the Mother of God spreads the Pokrov to shelter and protect the citizens of Constantinople from their enemies. Under her stands the fifth-century saint Romanos the Melode, who was the author of hymns dedicated to the Mother of God; to his right, stand St. Andrew the Holy Fool and his disciple Epiphanios, who were present during the miraculous appearance of the Mother of God.

The icon *St. Basil* (cat. no. 106, fig. 4) from the collections provides interesting historical information, since St. Basil is depicted standing in Red Square in front of the Cathedral of the Intercession and the Kremlin, showing how these buildings looked in the eighteenth century when this icon was painted.

Among the liturgical books in the Cathedral's collections is a Gospel from 1692 (cat. no. 351), which is beautifully covered in brocade with oklads, gilt silver plaques, and images of the Evangelists and the Resurrection. Besides books, the collection includes manuscripts on the lives of the saints from the sixteenth and seventeenth centuries.

Donations to the Cathedral include a remarkable silver chalice of 1638 (cat. no. 174). One of the inscriptions on the chalice says that it was donated by Tsar Michael Fedorovich, who was the first tsar of the Romanov dynasty.

This important monument of Russian architecture has always been haunted by the legend that Ivan the Terrible had the architects' eyes put out lest they create another church equally beautiful in another location. ❖

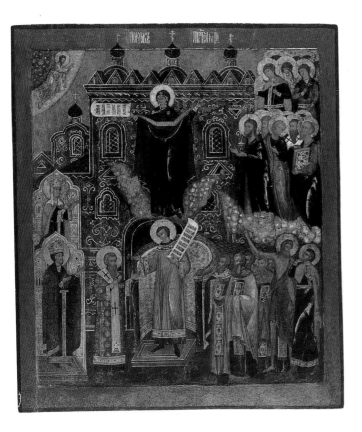

FIG. 3
*The Intercession of
the Mother of God*

FIG. 4
*St. Basil with the
Cathedral of the
Intercession and the
Moscow Kremlin in
the Background*

FIG. 1
Icon of the Crucifixion

FIG. 2
Icon of the
Last Judgement

FIG. 3
Icon of the Entry
into Jerusalem

ICON PAINTING

I. M. SHVEDOVA

It was in icons that the people of Russia found answers about their faith. The fact that a number of icon painters were canonized by the Orthodox Church indicates the importance and the deep meaning attached to these works.

Because of the wholesale destruction wrought by the Mongols in the thirteenth century, fewer than thirty icons from the early period of Russian Christianity survive. The period between the eleventh and thirteenth centuries saw the disintegration of Russian unity and the deliberate cultural isolation of the principalities from one another, as evidenced in the varied regional characteristics of these early paintings.

By the fourteenth century, the icons of Novgorod emerged as distinct expressions of Russian church art, recognizable by their sense of monumentality, even in moderately scaled works. St. George was a popular subject of veneration, and the artists of Novgorod produced many images of his life and martyrdom (cat. no. 104). Small, intimate icons, with very bright contrasting colors, and icons dedicated to saints, but bearing the names of family members of the donors, were also characteristic of work by Novgorod artists.

The size of Russian icons is indicative of their function. Small works were generally kept in monastery cells, in family chapels, or in private homes. Larger icons were placed in *kiots* (wall cases or niches) of churches or in prominent open locations. The frequent subjects were the Crucifixion (cat. no. 46, fig. 1) and the Last Judgment (cat. no. 111, fig. 2), instructing believers of their Christian duties. Icons also often contained didactic vignettes surrounding the central subject of the painting.

An iconostasis is a screen of icons used in Russian Orthodox churches to separate the sanctuary from the nave of the church. It can be arranged in as many as five tiers. The upper two tiers are associated with the prophecy of the birth of Christ, the Virgin, the Trinity, and the Old Testament Prophets, while the lower tiers contain large images of the apostles, saints, and prominent figures of the New Testament. In early versions of the Orthodox iconostasis, three upper tiers were used: the Deesis, the Last Judgment, and the Festival, which had images of the annual Feasts of the Church (cat. no. 43, fig. 3). The lowest tier, the Local, had images of the patron saint of the church and icons of Christ, the Mother of God, and other saints. (Icons from the iconostasis of the Mother of God of Smolensk Cathedral in the Novodevichy Convent are on view in this exhibition.[1])

In the medieval period, schools of icon painting developed in Moscow, Rostov-Suzdal, Novgorod, Tver, and other towns. With

1. It should be noted that the ceiling height in the exhibition space precluded a correct configuration of the iconostasis.

the unification of the Russian principalities around Moscow during the fifteenth century, the differences between schools of icon painting became less pronounced. War and fire had destroyed virtually all examples by Moscow painters of the twelfth and thirteenth centuries, and the influence of Byzantine artists could be seen in Russian icons at the beginning of the fourteenth century. Because of good relations with the Byzantine Empire, Moscow princes invited Greek masters to create frescoes and icons for Russian churches. Theophanes the Greek was the principal Byzantine icon painter working in Moscow during the fourteenth century. In the decades around 1400, the Moscow school of icon painting reached its zenith with the work of Andrei Rublev. A century later, the painter Dionysius became another major influence in the Moscow school.

In the fifteenth and sixteenth centuries, Russian princes, and particularly the first Russian tsar, Ivan the Terrible, continued to invite craftsmen and artists from other cities to build and decorate churches in Moscow. The Armory Chamber, with workshops for craftsmen, was founded by Ivan to carry out royal commissions. An outstanding master active in the Armory was icon painter Simon Ushakov (1626-1686), who executed a great many commissions, although conservative church officials took a dim view of the unorthodox influences in his work. His illustrations for books show the influence of European art on his style.

Ushakov painted the *Icon of the Seventh Ecumenical Council* for the Smolensk Cathedral in the Novodevichy Convent (cat. no. 85, fig. 4). The subject of the icon is the Council of Nicaea in 787, which affirmed the veneration of images.[2]

At the end of the seventeenth century, an icon workshop was established in Moscow that was associated with the state's ambassadorial service. Pupils were taught by foreign masters and sometimes traveled to study in Ukraine, which was under strong Polish cultural influence. An important painter from that workshop was Karp Zolotarev, who was commissioned to produce important iconostases, such as those for the Assumption and Transfiguration churches at Novodevichy. In 1685, Peter the Great's sister Sophia, Regent of Russia at the time, commissioned Zolotarev to create the icon *Faith, Hope, Love, and Their Mother Sophia* (cat. no. 94, fig. 5) for the St. Sophia Chapel of the Smolensk Cathedral in the Novodevichy Convent. ❖

2. The decision of the Second Council of Nicaea was reaffirmed at the Council of Constantinople in 843, bringing to an end the Iconoclastic controversy and the proscription on icons which had been declared in 726.

FIG. 4
*Icon of the Seventh
Ecumenical Council*

FIG. 5
*Icon of Faith, Hope,
Love, and Their
Mother Sophia*

FIG. 1
Cross

FIG. 2
Icon of the Cross

O. B. STRUGOVA

RUSSIAN WOODEN ICONS AND RELIGIOUS SCULPTURE

A collection of Russian religious objects carved in wood began to be amassed by the State Historical Museum during the nineteenth century. Many pieces were found in church basements or in the attics of homes, where they had been hidden each time a ban on three-dimensional religious imagery was imposed by Orthodox Church authorities.

Carved icons and sculpture have received less scholarly attention than other Russian church art, and because these icons have seldom been displayed in exhibitions, the assumption has been that they are less typical than other forms of Orthodox Church art. In truth, there is a rich tradition in Russia of carved religious objects with a variety of subjects.

The origin of religious sculpture and images in relief goes back to the pre-Christian era. Traditional pagan art and rituals influenced and were incorporated into the practices of the early-Christians. In fact, pagan wood carvings continued to be revered as sacred objects for centuries after Christianity was brought to Russia. In the early-Christian period, stone crosses were often worshiped. It is thought that these large crosses, many of which are still preserved in the northwest of Russia, were erected on the sites of pagan temples and that devotion to these crosses may have been linked to pagan rituals. Worship of these crosses tended to be associated with some miraculous event, such as a healing of disease or rescue from a shipwreck.

Out of this tradition came carved wooden icons depicting the Cross. Most were carved in monasteries, particularly in the northern provinces of Russia. (See cat. no. 133, fig. 1, and cat. no. 79, fig. 2, for good examples.)

It should be noted, that many aspects of the earliest icons were preserved up through the nineteenth century. Traditions from early-Christian and even pre-Christian religious art can be seen in the style of much later religious objects.

In Novgorod from the thirteenth to the fifteenth century, many icons depicting the Holy Sepulcher in Jerusalem were carved. Frequent pilgrimages to the Holy Land made the Holy Sepulcher a popular subject, but it can also be seen as connected with traditional depictions of the Church.

Throughout Russia, early Deeses were frequently carved. Next to the usual symmetrical compositions of Christ with the Mother of God and John the Baptist, the Archangels, and the Apostles, many carvers added local patron saints. In examples from northern Russia, these compositions tended to be asymmetrical.

While northern carved icons were often folk art, and as such, rather primitive and crude, a number of works in this exhibition should be noted for their remarkably fine quality. Among them is a portion of a seventeenth-century Deesis with six figures (see cat. nos. 137-142, fig. 3). The carving and painted decoration suggest it was made in a northern monastery, and its relationship to painted icons is evident. Other carved objects in the exhibition also show the influence of painted icons, such as *The Saints of*

FIG. 3
Six figures from a Deesis

FIG. 4
Icon of the Saints of Rostov and St. Nicholas the Miracle Worker

Rostov and St. Nicholas the Miracle Worker (cat. no. 15, fig. 4), a sixteenth-century work, and the rare *Dormition of the Mother of God* (cat. no. 110, fig. 5). One of the oldest carved icons in the State Historical Museum is the *Archangel Michael* (cat. no. 10, fig. 6), an early-sixteenth-century work notable for its detail. Small elaborate carvings like this show the influence of Eastern European art from Byzantium. Contrary to earlier opinions, wooden images of saints did appear before the sixteenth century. Such images began to be produced in Moscow in the fourteenth and fifteenth centuries. Moscow had become one of the leading cultural centers in Russia by that time, and its artistic influence soon spread to other regions. Among the more popular images of saints depicted by woodcarvers were St. Nicholas the Miracle Worker, St. George, and the Archangel Michael.

One of the best preserved carvings of St. Nicholas the Miracle Worker (cat. no. 67, fig. 7) was made in the seventeenth century. The Saint holds a model of the town of Mozhaysk in the left hand with a sword (now lost) in the other. Similar images became popular throughout Russia as icons of protection.

The use of wooden sculpture in religious art spread in Russia during the seventeenth and eighteenth centuries with urban growth and the construction and renovation of churches. At the same time, the growing influence of western art brought a new style, European Baroque, which was much less static than the earlier Russian style and lent itself to being used as decorative elements in the architecture of the iconostasis. By the end of the eighteenth century, both styles of sculpture were being employed across Russia for different purposes: The works created in the old traditions used for religious icons, the new western Baroque style used for architectural decoration.

The iconostasis itself went through major changes in style. Prior to the seventeenth century its construction was based on horizontal beams, painted or carved in low relief, separating the tiers of icons. By the end of the seventeenth-century deep carvings decorated the beams of the iconostasis, and there was

FIG. 5
*Icon of the Dormition
of the Mother of God*

FIG. 6
*Icon of the Archangel
Michael*

FIG. 7
*Icon of St. Nicholas the
Miracle Worker*

increasing use of decorative sculpture depicting angels and other holy figures.

The Royal Doors of the iconostasis were given special emphasis. The Doors in the exhibition (cat. no. 159) are among the masterpieces of Russian ecclesiastical sculpture and a fine example of the Baroque influence. They were carved in north-central Russia in the second half of the eighteenth century.

Russian Orthodox Church authorities had denounced the three-dimensional wooden depictions of saints as being equal to pagan idols, but before the early eighteenth century, only hollow statues were completely banned from being placed in the churches. After 1722, decrees were issued periodically prohibiting any sculptural images of saints from being displayed in churches.

Carved images of the Crucifixion, on the other hand, were permitted, and during the eighteenth century became obligatory for ceremonial purposes. They were often placed on top of the multi-tiered iconostasis, although this too was frowned upon by church authorities lest they fall off and injure the clergy or congregation.

Ultimately, sculptural images continued to be carved by Russian artists throughout the central and northern provinces, in spite of the injunctions against them. The rich beautiful woods found in Russia were too compelling to be ignored by her artists.
❖

T. I. SIZOVA

RUSSIAN LITURGICAL METALWORK AND JEWELRY FROM THE TWELFTH TO THE TWENTIETH CENTURY

FIG. 1

A. *Pectoral Icon of the Descent into Hell*

B. *Pectoral Icon of the Mother of God Hodegitria*

C. *Pectoral Icon of the Holy Sepulcher*

D. *Pectoral Icon of the Archangel Michael and John the Baptist*

E. *Pectoral Icon of Warrior Saints George and Fedor Stratilat*

The finest work of early Russian gold and silversmiths was directly and indirectly associated with the Russian Orthodox Church, which became the focus of all creative activity. Russian church art descended from Byzantine traditions, since liturgical works by artists from Constantinople had come to Russia with the clergy when the country was Christianized in the tenth century.

The rulers of Kiev invited Greek artists to come there and establish workshops, and from these Greek masters, their Russian pupils learned techniques, as well as thematic and symbolic content, which they then adapted to the established traditions of eastern Slavic metalwork. The artifacts found by archaeologists show a clear reliance on Byzantine models. Yet, the spiritual content and the style of work by Russian craftsmen did not suffer in comparison with their Byzantine masters. Comparisons made by contemporaries of Russian masters with their Near Eastern and European counterparts were favorable, although we cannot accept them uncritically without knowing more of early Russian church art, and regrettably, so much of it was lost to fire and wars.

In spite of the continued political upheavals in Russia between the thirteenth and early seventeenth centuries, metalsmithing and jewelry-making techniques continued to develop, and new artistic centers were established. The work of craftsmen from Novgorod, Tver, Pskov, and Moscow was particularly notable for the individual styles and ornamentation. Their achievements can be seen in the earliest objects in this exhibition (see cat. nos. 1, 2, 4, 6, 7, fig. 1, and cat. nos. 19, 20, fig. 2). These small-scale objects carved from wood, stone, and bone, and embellished with gold and silver, usually depicted saints or crosses. They were often related to folk art, and Russian attitudes toward these sacred objects created a tradition of veneration of these family relics.

A.

B.

C.

E.

D.

The city of Novgorod, which accepted Christianity at the same time as Kiev, became the largest economic and political center in the earliest period of the newly embraced faith. The city was spared devastation by the Crusaders in the thirteenth century and also the scourge of the Mongol invasion. Archaeological excavations of sites dating from the eleventh to the fourteenth century show Novgorod as an important center of metal and jewelry production. The objects created by Novgorod craftsmen were of high technical achievement and expressive originality, yet showed a pronounced adherence to old Slavic heritage and Scandinavian and Byzantine traditions.

These works depict a wide variety of themes. Craftsmen from Novgorod were especially fond of subjects such as the Holy Sepulcher, the Crucifixion, St. Nicholas, and St. George the Bearer of Victory. In Moscow, favored subjects included the Mother of God, the Savior, and the Old Testament Trinity. Most frequent of all were the depictions of the protector saints of Russian warriors in works from the thirteenth to the sixteenth centuries.

Gold and silver church art increased dramatically after the country was freed from the Mongols in 1480 and the Russian state was established. With Moscow now the capital of Russia, master craftsmen flocked to that city from Novgorod, Pskov, the Volga River towns, the northern provinces, and the southern borders. Greek, Italian, and German masters were invited to come to Moscow and contributed greatly to the Russian art of metalsmithing and jewelry-making.

Church construction in Moscow, which increased in the fifteenth and sixteenth centuries, led to increased production of liturgical artifacts. The four most important cathedrals inside the Kremlin were built within thirty years, including the great Cathedral of the Assumption, which was erected between 1475 and 1479. It became the burial place of Russian metropolitans and patriarchs, and it was here that the coronations and weddings of the princes and later the tsars and emperors of Russia took place.

The decoration of new churches and the growing complexity and richness of the Orthodox liturgy created a demand for objects for liturgical use. They were produced by craftsmen in the Kremlin workshops and in monasteries. The style of silversmiths in

FIG. 2
Icon of "We Rejoice in Thee"

Small Folding Icon with Scenes of the Crucifixion, the Apostles, the Old Testament Trinity, and the Mother of God of the Sign

FIG. 3
Censer

FIG. 4
Icon of the Mother of God
Appearing to St. Sergius

Fig. 5
Small Icon in the
Shape of a Flower

Fig. 6
Altar Cross

Novgorod greatly influenced the style of church objects made in Moscow. By combining this influence from Novgorod with their own advances and styles, Moscow artists of the fifteenth and sixteenth centuries became the leading silversmiths of Russia.

The flourishing production of gold and silver objects in Moscow during the sixteenth century became associated with the Kremlin workshops, especially the new Armory Chamber. The Chamber created some of the most important and beautiful religious objects in Russia. The censer of 1597 (cat. no. 169, fig. 3) and the oklad of the icon *The Mother of God Appears to St. Sergius* (cat. no. 23, fig. 4) are excellent examples.

Objects of the finest quality were also characteristic of the northern provinces, especially in Solvychegodsk. The Stroganov family of merchants and industrialists, who played an important part in the development of the natural treasures of Siberia and the north, is connected with the development of particularly fine crafts and icon paintings from this region. Examples of work by northern silversmiths during the sixteenth century are rare, and were generally found only as unique pieces in the treasuries of tsars, patriarchs, and the aristocracy.

The gold and silversmiths of the seventeenth century were worthy successors of earlier artists. They continued to combine new styles with traditional forms, and their daring interpretations of both western European and Near Eastern themes became characteristic of religious and secular art objects of this time. Oriental influences on Russian metalwork were extensive during the latter half of the seventeenth century, but it did not have much lasting effect.

Moscow remained the artistic center throughout this century, with the most skillful craftsmen active in the Armory Chamber. A diamond-studded panagia in the form of a flower (cat. no. 88, fig. 5) and an altar cross, made in 1694, that belonged to the mother of Peter the Great (cat. no. 199, fig. 6) demonstrate the artistry of Moscow jewelers from this period.

From the mid-fifteenth century on, enamel was the most extensively used decorative technique. The miter made in 1685 at the Kremlin workshops on the order of the co-tsars Ivan V and Peter I and their sister Sophia is an exceptionally fine example (cat. no. 337, front cover).

Church art decorated with niello work was particularly popular. The technique was well known to the old Slavic craftspeople, whose work rivaled the pieces imported from Byzantium. Niello began to be used extensively in Russia in the fifteenth century, and in the centuries following, Moscow workers achieved high

FIG. 8
Chalice and
Plate with Agnus Dei

FIG. 9
Basin for Holy Water

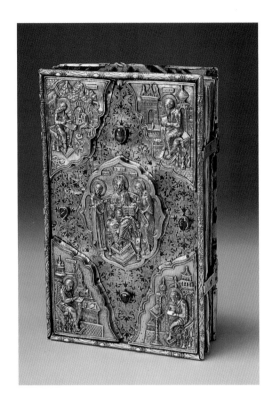

levels of proficiency in it. The cover of a seventeenth century Gospel from the time of Ivan the Terrible (cat. no. 347, fig. 7) is a splendid example in its combination of niello with chased images and precious stones. The chalice and plate of 1686 (cat. nos. 190, 191, fig. 8) and the basin for holy water of 1693 (cat. no. 197, fig. 9) are also fine examples of this technique.

Growing contacts with western Europe during the eighteenth century exposed Russian artists and craftspeople to the Baroque, and created the problem of blending two unrelated styles. Neither Russian painting nor the crafts ever comfortably combined these styles.

The discovery of precious metal deposits in the Urals and in Siberia in the early eighteenth century accelerated the production of Russian metal objects. This era was marked by a European-influenced style, which became known in Russia as Peter's Baroque, and in the following generation as Elizabeth's Baroque, after the Empress Elizabeth, Peter's daughter.

French Neo-Classicism deeply influenced Russian art well into the nineteenth century. As in the West, eclecticism became fashionable during the nineteenth century, and artists drew on old Russian traditions, as well as the foreign influences.

With technical advances in the metal and jewelry industry, handcrafted work merged into factory production, as in the firms of Sazikov, Goubkin, Nemirov-Kolodkin, Olovianishnikov, and Fabergé. The firm of Fabergé, which became the most famous and admired of the new companies, contributed to the design and manufacture of religious art, as well as fabulous bibelots. This exhibition includes a gold cross fashioned by the brilliant Fabergé masters August Hollming and Fedor Rückert (cat. no. 239, fig. 10). ✣

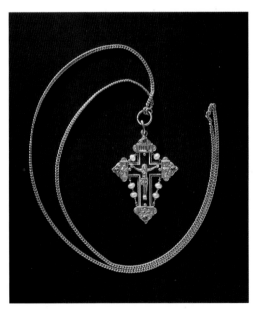

Fig. 7
Gospel with Oklad

Fig. 10
Personal Cross with Chain

40

ORNAMENTAL EMBROIDERY AND CHURCH VESTMENTS

L. V. EFIMOVA AND O. G. GORDEEVA

Archaeological excavations in Russia have brought to light many pre-Christian Slavic examples of embroidery with silk, gold, and silver threads. When Christianity came to Russia as its official religion in 988, church building began on a grand scale. The sumptuous interiors of these Orthodox churches and the ever more elaborate liturgical rites created a great demand for textiles, including altar cloths, wall hangings, icon draperies, shrouds, and vestments. Embroidered in gold and silver thread and studded with pearls and sparkling gems, these splendid textiles added to the beauty of the churches and to their emotional appeal.

As with all early-Christian art in Russia, embroidery was heavily influenced by Byzantine artists, but gradually the Byzantine influence was replaced with a more Russian style. Although very few of the earliest textiles survive, some figural embroideries of saints and biblical scenes remain. Most of the examples we have today were made from the fifteenth through the seventeenth centuries.

In medieval Russia, women from prosperous households often excelled at embroidery. *Domostroi*, a sixteenth-century treatise on everyday life and morals, listed needlework among a woman's cardinal virtues, and Russian homes usually included a spacious, well-lit area in the women's quarters for needlework and dressmaking. Embroidery was added to festive garments and home decorations, as well as church textiles. Very large articles, such as a shroud, required the work of several women at once and often took several years to complete.

Sophisticated representations required preliminary designs by professional icon painters and calligraphers, either by means of outlines on waxed paper or chalk marks directly on the fabric. One artist might create the central image, another the floral designs and borders, and a calligrapher the inscriptions. But it was the embroiderer who selected the stitch, the color scheme, and the cloth, and ultimately it was her personality, taste, and craftsmanship that determined the artistic and emotional impact of the piece.

Figural embroidery required the use of fine silk, lined with linen and stretched on a frame. Faces were made in satin stitch with silk thread covering the whole surface. Gold and silver threads were placed in parallel rows and attached with silk thread. Buttonhole and other stitches were used for additional details. Russian embroidery was rightfully referred to as "needle painting."

Russia imported silks from Persia, Turkey, and China. Italian velvets and brocades were extremely popular, as were large-

FIG. 1
*Icon Drapery with
the Apostle Phillip*

FIG. 2
*Altar Cloth with the
Mother of God of the Sign*

patterned silk damasks. Red damask was widely used with gold embroidery. Gold thread and fine yarns also came from the Orient. An early account says that German craftsmen began producing gold and silver thread in Moscow's royal workshops in the early seventeenth century, but it also refers to a Russian wire-drawer active in the 1620s.

The style of Russian embroidery was, of course, part and parcel of Russia's cultural developments, following its traditions right to the end of the nineteenth century.

One of the finest embroideries from the Moscow school is an icon drapery (podea) with an image of the Apostle Phillip, dating from the 1590s (cat. no. 245, fig. 1). The piece is attributed to the workshop supervised by Matrëna, the wife of Dimitry Godunov, uncle of Tsar Boris Godunov. The Godunov embroidery workshop, which reached its height at the end of the century, used designs by royal icon painters. Also attributed to the Godunov workshop is an altar cloth (aer) from 1606 (cat. no. 248, fig. 2), which was donated to the St. Euphemia Monastery in Suzdal. The inscriptions and figures on the cloth are meticulously outlined in pearls, which probably would have come from the Orient or northern Russia.

Depictions the Mother of God with Christ were particularly venerated, and two versions on icon draperies of very different styles are included in the exhibition. The icon drapery with the Mother of God of Grebnev (cat. no. 246, fig. 3) is embroidered in silk with a multi-colored inscription and a border of patterned silk. The icon drapery with the Kazan Mother of God (cat. no. 264, fig. 4), on the other hand, mimics an oklad of precious metals with its mass of gold and silver threads stitched over with silk thread.

Many cloths represented St. Nicholas, one of Russia's favorite saints, patron of the poor and protector in shipwrecks, disease, and war. Travelers often carried icons or the more portable embroidered cloths bearing his image. An embroidered icon drapery of St. Nicholas (cat. no. 291, fig. 5) is included in the exhibition.

The first Russian silk manufacturers emerged in the era of Peter the Great (ruled 1682–1725). A mill was established in St. Petersburg in 1714, and three years later one was started in Moscow. By mid-century, many textile manufacturers were operating in Russia, producing satin, grisette, taffeta, gros de tours, and brocade of a quality that rivaled the fabrics of Europe. Moscow was the heart of this industry throughout the eighteenth century, and by the turn of the century, 210 mills were manufacturing silk in the city. The establishment of schools for textile design contributed to the industry; the first school was opened in 1831

Fig. 3
*Icon Drapery with the
Mother of God of
Grebnev*

Fig. 4
*Icon Drapery with the
Kazan Mother of God*

Fig. 5
*Icon Drapery with
St. Nicholas the Miracle
Worker*

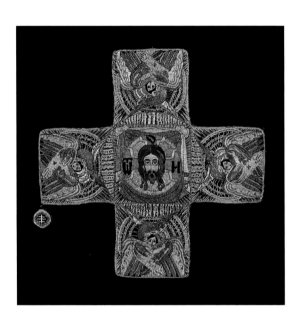

by the Gerasimov brothers.

The Sapozhnikov brocade mill was one of the best known in the nineteenth century. The company took part in all national expositions and those abroad, consistently winning gold medals for excellence. In 1896, the company was chosen to weave brocades in traditional designs for the coronation of Nicholas II.

Russian liturgical embroideries from the late nineteenth and early twentieth centuries have never been shown in America, and they have never been exhibited in the State Historical Museum. They have been given scholarly attention only recently because of a renewed interest in this period known as the Russian Silver Age, distinguished by an eclectic mixing of traditional techniques with modern styles (cat. no. 324, fig. 6, and cat. no. 325, fig. 7). The State Historical Museum's holdings in this area were drawn from the Olovianishnikov Collection, the Armory Chamber of the Kremlin, and from the Donskoy Monastery.

The Olovianishnikovs were manufacturers and the publishers of *The Luminary*, a periodical distinguished for its graphic design and content, which presented discussions and illustrations of the finest examples of Byzantine and Russian medieval art. The editorial board included renowned historians, art historians, writers, and artists.

The Royal Stroganov School of Art also encouraged its students to study Russian art history and began to train them in medieval design and craftsmanship. An icon painting workshop was started in 1904, and students' studies and dissertations began to focus on liturgical objects, such as embroidered cloths and vestments. The famous painter Michael Vrubel was a faculty member the Stroganov School.

Olovianishnikov & Sons, which began production in an old bell foundry in 1901, brought Russian brocade its final triumphs, creating liturgical objects such as embroidered cloths, icons, and other textiles (cat. no. 321, fig. 8). Principal factories were established in Moscow, Yaroslavl, and St. Petersburg, with branches operating throughout Russia. Sergey Vashkov, a graduate from the Stroganov School and a prominent artist, was among its principal designers. A great collector and scholar of antique church objects, Vashkov's designs for the company sought to revive traditional styles and techniques in modern forms.

The Russian Silver Age, with its emphasis on medieval arts and crafts, created a renewed interest in embroidery. Traditional techniques and patterns were combined with new elements, such as beads and colored glass (cat. no. 326, fig. 9). ❖

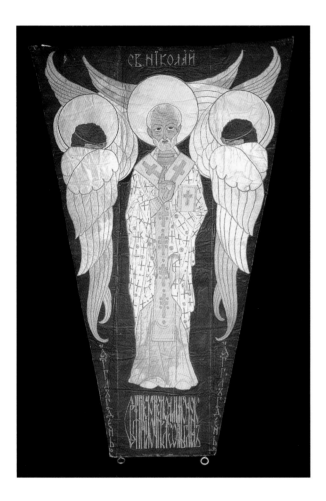

FIG. 7
*Processional Cloth
with St. Nicholas*

FIG. 8
Shroud

FIG. 9
*Icon Drapery with
St. Efrem*

FIG. 1
Mstislav Gospel

FIG. 2
Andronikov Gospel

RUSSIAN MANUSCRIPTS
AND PRINTED BOOKS

E. V. SHULGINA

The oldest examples of Russian manuscripts date back to the eleventh century, and this art form relates to the stylistic characteristics of both frescoes and icon painting. Books from the eleventh to the fourteenth centuries were written on vellum with goose quills and ferrous inks made from plant extracts and iron filings. Miniatures were painted with organic and mineral media, decorated with gold and silver leaf. The covers consisted of wooden boards covered with leather and metal bindings. Altar gospels were lavishly decorated with gems and precious metals.

By the end of the fourteenth century, paper gradually replaced costly vellum, a change which greatly affected the character of books and manuscripts. With watercolor replacing the miniaturist's egg-based colors, combined with the delicate ivory tones of paper, the decoration of illuminated manuscripts took on a new and different quality.

This exhibition includes modern copies of two early manuscripts: The Mstislav Gospel suggests Byzantine influences (cat. no. 346, fig. 1), and the Andronikov Gospel (cat. no. 340, fig. 2), shows the influence of the great painter Andrei Rublev, who was so important in the early fifteenth century.

The very fine fifteenth-century manuscript the *Acts of the Apostles* (cat. no. 343) includes six miniatures of the Apostles, painted in brilliant colors against a gold background and marked by a new narrative element, a pronounced departure from previous iconography.

The sixteenth century produced a number of illuminated Psalters. The Godunov Psalter (cat. no. 342) was ordered by the boyar Dimitry Godunov from the Kremlin scriptorium, to be donated to major monasteries and principal cathedrals in Moscow. The narrative miniatures are remarkable illustrations of the text and echo the images of the iconostasis in the Mother of God of Smolensk Cathedral at the Novodevichy Convent.

Book printing first appeared in Russia during the reign of Ivan the Terrible, in 1564, under the sponsorship of the Metropolitan Macarius. The *Acts of the Apostles* (cat. no. 341) was the first book to be printed by official order. According to its colophon, it was produced by the Moscow Court Press, founded by Ivan Fedorov and Peter Mstislavets. The design and decoration of this book includes an engraved frontispiece of St. Luke and rivals the finest manuscripts.

The Bible of 1663 (cat. no. 348), printed by the Moscow Printing Press, includes an engraving of an intricate composition by the artist Zosimas, made during the time of Tsar Alexis

Mikhailovich, the father of Peter the Great. The center of the engraving shows an image of the tsar smiting a dragon which adorns the breast of a double-headed eagle. Below is a map of Moscow, and scriptural scenes decorate the margins.

Many interesting and beautiful books were published by the Upper Printing Press of Moscow in the seventeenth century. They were edited and published by the prominent ecclesiastic and politician, Simon Polotsky. Among his works was a version of the Psalms in rhyme, which he published in 1680 with an engraving and decorations by the artist Afanasi Trukhmensky (cat. no. 350).

Important documents were printed according to special design standards which reflected the patterns of old manuscripts. The deed of 1672 on the patriarchal appointment of the Metropolitan Pitirim is a fine example with its festive and impressive design (catalogue no. 345).

The subjects of publications printed over the centuries were varied. Many secular books appeared in the seventeenth century, including books of titulars, such as the one printed in the late seventeenth century and included in this exhibition (cat. no. 353). The book includes watercolor portraits of Russian princes and tsars (from Rurik to Ivan Alexeevich), patriarchs, and foreign royalty, all framed in floral patterns and gold decoration.

The introduction of hagiography produced illustrated accounts of the lives of saints with narrative illustrations. Among the most widely read was the *Life of Zossima and Savvatii of the Solovetsk Monastery*, which described the history of the Solovetsk Monastery in the north of Russia and the colonization of the White Sea coast. The seventeenth-century copy in the exhibition (cat. no. 344) is illustrated with superb miniatures and unique baroque decorations.

The *Life of St. Basil the Blessed*, the saint who was so highly venerated in Moscow, was compiled after 1588, the year when his remains were exhumed. The copy of the book in the exhibition (cat. no. 359), dating from 1790, is illustrated with miniatures and vignettes reminiscent of folk art.

From the seventeenth to the nineteenth centuries, various decorative patterns were developed and used in book designs. The *Life of Prince Vladimir* (cat. no. 360) is decorated with sumptuous patterns which are a synthesis of folk traditions in a style unique to the area of the White Sea. Similar motifs known as *guslitsky* because they emerged in Guslitsy, a community of deeply conservative Russians, are found in the Octoechos, a book of liturgical songs (cat. no. 362, fig. 3). Many pages are covered in patterns of luscious flowers and foliage with glowing colors. Musical

FIG. 3
Music for the Holidays

FIG. 4
Anthology

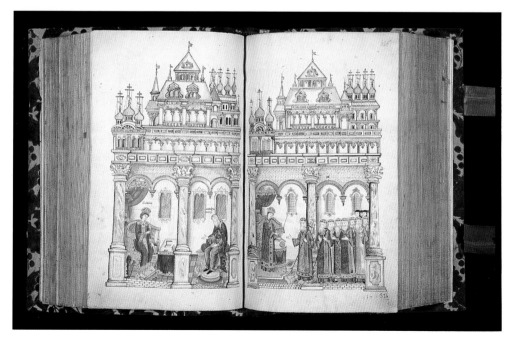

notations are gracefully added above the texts.

The Anthology of 1765 (cat. no. 357, fig. 4) is in the style of medieval book illuminations with its twelve watercolor miniatures of Moscow cathedrals and the Kremlin. In two of them, Ivan the Terrible and the Metropolitan Macarius are depicted in the ornate chambers of the Kremlin.

The illustrations for the *Life of Tsar Peter I* by his contemporary Peter Krekshin (cat. no. 354) are similar to prints by folk artists. The pages are adorned with garlands of flowers and medallions and scenes of contemporary life. The ornate script of the text blends freely with the decoration.

Manuscript and book design reflected the spiritual wealth of Russia and the visual traditions. The designs responded to the needs of all social strata from the early centuries to recent times. ❖

CATALOGUE OF THE EXHIBITION

Information about the works in the exhibition is based on material provided by the curators of the State Historical Museum and translated in Moscow. Dimensions are given in centimeters, height precedes width precedes depth. Where it is known, the artist is listed after the title and date. A manufacturer or workshop, followed by the city is listed next, and finally, the medium and dimensions.

CAT. NO. 9

ICONS

1. **PECTORAL ICON OF THE DESCENT INTO HELL (ANASTASIS)**, 11th-12th century
Byzantium
Jasper, carving
6.2 x 4.9
Illustrated on page 35
GIM 53151/73, OK 10965 (269)

2. **PECTORAL ICON OF WARRIOR SAINTS GEORGE AND FEDOR STRATILAT**, 12th century
Byzantium
Steatite, carving
9.9 x 8.3
Illustrated on page 35
GIM 77091, OK 13176 (270)

    Acquired from the collection of Count A. S. Uvarov, the first director of the Museum, in 1921.

3. **PECTORAL ICON OF THE MOTHER OF GOD AND THE INFANT CHRIST**, 12th-13th century
Russia
Silver and copper alloy, casting
6 x 5
GIM 67507, OK 6046 (271)

    First publication.

4. **PECTORAL ICON OF THE HOLY SEPULCHER**, 12th-13th century
Novgorod
Slate, silver
8.4 x 7
Illustrated on page 35
GIM 54626, OK 9198 (272)

    Depictions of the Holy Sepulcher, signifying Christ's divine nature and His resurrection, were very popular in Novgorod in the 12th and 13th centuries. Byzantine icons were used as prototypes for Russian stone icons like this one.

    Acquired from the Rumiantsev Museum (Egorov Collection) in 1923.

5. **ICON OF THE CRUCIFIXION WITH ST. GEORGE, ST. ELIJAH, ST. NICHOLAS, AND ST. BARBARA**, 14th century
Northern Province
Wood, carving
25.5 x 22.8 x 7
GIM 42350/1410 (147)

6. **PECTORAL ICON OF THE MOTHER OF GOD HODEGITRIA**, 14th century
Moscow
Slate, silver, gilt, filigree, carving
6.4 x 5.5
Illustrated on page 35
GIM 4814 shch, OK 9213 (273)

    This image of the Virgin with the Infant Christ is notable for its elaborately carved faces with distinctive features, the detailed folds in the clothing, and the ornamented halos.
    Acquired from the collection of P. I. Shchukin in 1905.

7. **PECTORAL ICON OF THE ARCHANGEL MICHAEL AND JOHN THE BAPTIST**, late 14th–early 15th century
Novgorod
Shale, silver, gilt, semi-precious stones, glass, carving, filigree
9.5 x 6.9 x .7
Illustrated on page 35
GIM 4860 shch, OK 9107 (274)

    Acquired from the P. I. Shchukin collection in 1905.

8. **ICON OF JOHN THE BAPTIST (JOHN THE FORERUNNER)**, late 14th–early 15th century
Oklad, 16th century
Wood, gesso, tempera, silver, gilt, niello, engraving, embossing
47.5 x 38
GIM 103803, NDM 3314/870, SV-802 (32)

    This icon was a personal possession of Tsaritsa Irina Godunov.

9. **ICON OF THE GREAT MARTYR ST. PARASKEVA PIATNITSA**, early 16th century
Northern Province
Wood, gesso, tempera
59.3 x 41.2
Illustrated on page 51
GIM 58271, IUSH 223 (132)

CAT. NO. 16

CAT. NO. 17

10. ICON OF THE ARCHANGEL MICHAEL,
early 16th century
Central Russia
Cypress, limewood, tempera, traces
of gilt, carving
37.5 x 30.5 x 4
Illustrated on page 33
GIM 7975/270 (181)

11. ICON OF THE TIKHVIN MOTHER
OF GOD, 16th century
Novgorod
Wood, gesso, tempera
184 x 135 x 4.5
GIM 103803, NDM 1727/1289 (40)

From the Cathedral of the Mother of
God of Smolensk in the Novodevichy
Convent in Moscow.

12. ICON OF THE MOTHER OF GOD
HODEGITRIA WITH SAINTS, 16th
century
Moscow
Carved wood, tempera
38.5 x 26 cm.
GIM 103794/819 (123)

This image is a type called
Hodegitria, which in Greek means
"showing the way." The Mother of
God gestures toward the Christ Child
with her right hand, indicating that
He is the way to salvation.

13. ICON OF ST. BASIL THE GREAT,
ST. NICHOLAS, ST. JOHN THE BAPTIST,
AND LEV THE PATRIARCH, 16th century
Novgorod
Wood, gesso, tempera
58.9 x 46.9
GIM 85919, I VIII 4073 (126)

14. ICON OF THE MOTHER OF GOD
OF THE SIGN, FRONT; ICON OF
ST. NICHOLAS, BACK, 16th century
Wood, gesso, tempera
49.5 x 51 (without handle),
h. 154 (with handle)
GIM 58270, I VIII 2249 (131)

15. ICON OF THE SAINTS OF ROSTOV
AND ST. NICHOLAS THE MIRACLE
WORKER, 16th century
Rostov the Great
Wood, carving
19 x 17 x 1.7
Illustrated on page 32
GIM 2925 shch/284 (182)

16-17. LEAVES OF A FOLDING ICON
(SKLADEN) WITH THE OLD
TESTAMENT TRINITY AND THE
MOTHER OF GOD OF THE SIGN,
16th century
Wood, paint, carving
8.8 x 7.6 x 1
Illustrated on page 52
GIM 24807/797; GIM 24804/798 (197-198)

First publication.

18. DOUBLE-SIDED PECTORAL ICON OF
THE MOTHER OF GOD AND SAINTS,
16th century
Wood, silver, carving
9.7 x 6 x 1.2
GIM 68702/490 (200)

First publication.

19. ICON OF "WE REJOICE IN THEE,"
16th century
Moscow
Walrus bone, carving
11.7 x 9.1
Illustrated on page 36
GIM 3106 shch, OK 9273 (275)

Since ancient times, artists had used
bone to create objects, but the earliest surviving bone icons are dated
from the 14th and 15th centuries.
Walrus bone, a hard substance, was
widely used to produce crosses and
icons and lent itself to the carving of
complex multifigural compositions.

Acquired from the collection of
P. I. Shchukin in 1905.

20. Small Folding Icon (Panagia) with Scenes of the Crucifixion, the Apostles, the Old Testament Trinity, and the Mother of God of the Sign, 16th century
Oklad, 18th century
Probably Moscow
Walrus bone, silver, carving
Diam. 7.2
Illustrated on page 36
GIM 54626, OK 11553 (276)

A round two-sided folding icon, or panagia, was intended to be worn on the chest. Certain features of the carving, inscriptions, and images place this example within a group of artifacts created in the mid-16th century in and around Moscow. The figures depicted are from both the Old and New Testament.

21. Folding Icon-Shrine (Skladen), 16th century
Novgorod
Silver, wood, gilt, leather, iron, velvet, carving, filigree
23.5 x 41.7
GIM 54627, OK 10102 (279)

The icon of the Pantocrator forms the central part of the skladen, with images of the Mother of God and Fedor Tiron on the side panels. The presence of Fedor Tiron in the Deesis is very rare and suggests that he was probably the patron saint of a government official.
　　Acquired from the Rumiantsev Museum in 1923.

22. Icon of the Evangelist Mark, 16th century
Wood, silver, gilt, tempera, silver gilt, hand stamping, carving
33.7 x 28.3
GIM 75419, OK 8453 (300)

This icon of St. Mark is enhanced with an oklad, which, in technique and decoration, is typical of 16th-century church art.
　　Acquired from the Museum of Kostroma in 1933.

23. Icon of the Mother of God Appearing to St. Sergius, 16th century
Moscow
Wood, tempera, silver, gilt, almandines, hand stamping, filigree, carving
30.9 x 25.5
Illustrated on page 37
GIM 75399, OK 8293 (301)

The image of the Mother of God appearing to St. Sergius was a theme widely used in icon painting of the 16th century in Moscow and Novgorod. Its popularity may have been due to the particular representation of the Mother of God as Patroness of Russian lands and the Orthodox Church. St. Sergius of Radonezh (ca. 1321–1391), founder of the Monastery of the Holy Trinity, was an active proponent of Russian unification under the central authority of Moscow. He was canonized in 1422.

24. Icon of the Savior, 16th century
Novgorod
Wood, silver, enamel, tempera, fabric, filigree
30.3 x 25
GIM 74822, OK 8127 (303)

25. Icon of the Mother of God of the Sign and the Raising of the Cross, first half of the 16th century
Northern Province
Wood, gesso, tempera
55 x 51.8 (without handle), h. 131 (with handle)
GIM 16189 I VIII 3472, shch (134)

26. Icon of St. Basil the Great, St. Gregory the Theologian, and St. John Chrysostom, mid-16th century
Pskov
Wood, gesso, tempera, silver, niello
85.5 x 77.5
GIM 99727, I VIII 5880 (128)

27. Icon of the Descent into Hell (Anastasis), mid-16th century
Moscow
Wood, gesso, tempera
140.3 x 110
Illustrated on back cover
GIM 85762 I VIII 5293 (129)

28. Icon of the Miracle of St. George and the Dragon, second half of the 16th century
Novgorod
Wood, gesso, tempera
62.5 x 49.2
GIM 53159, I VIII 1219 (125)

This painting was cut from the original icon and set into a new panel.

29. Icon of the Old Testament Trinity, second half of the 16th century
Pskov
Wood, gesso, tempera
104.2 x 74.5
GIM 53054, I VIII 1591 (127)

30. Icon of the Mother of God of Tikhvin, second half of the 16th century
Moscow
Wood, gesso, tempera
69.6 x 48
GIM 58283, I VIII 1589 (130)

31. Icon of St. Athanasius of Alexandria, second half of the 16th century
Northern Province
Wood, gesso, tempera
50.5 x 36.9
GIM 54628, I VIII 1732 (133)

CAT. NO. 32A, B

32. LEAVES OF FOLDING ICON (SKLADEN) WITH SCENES FROM THE LIFE OF ST. NIKITA, 1595
Prokopy Chirin
Oklad, 1598 in Solvychegodsk
Wood, tempera, silver, gilt, enamel, niello, filigree
36.6 x 13.6 x 2.8 (each)
Illustrated on page 54
GIM 74873, OK 6065 (304)

33. ICON OF JOHN THE BAPTIST (JOHN THE FORERUNNER), late 16th century
Moscow
Wood, gesso, tempera, silver gilt, engraving
214 x 75 x 3.5
GIM 103803, NDM 6078/1496/40, SV-851 (3)

From the Deesis tier of the iconostasis of the Cathedral of the Mother of God of Smolensk in the Novodevichy Convent in Moscow.

34. ICON OF THE MOTHER OF GOD, late 16th century
Moscow
Oklad, mid-17th century in Veliky Ustiug
Wood, tempera, silver, pearls, stones, glass, textile, filigree, gilt, enamel
35 x 28
Illustrated on page 55
GIM 81365, OK 13922 (306)

The range of color in the enameling, the highly stylized ornamentation, and the unusual technique of laying enamel on metal surfaces exemplify the creative work of the jewelers of Veliky Ustiug in the 17th century.

Acquired through private purchase in 1944.

35. ICON OF THE SAINTS BORIS AND GLEB, late 16th-early 17th century
Moscow
Oklad, 1683
Wood, gesso, tempera, silver gilt, precious stones, embossing
160 x 116 x 4
GIM 103803, NDM 6078/1496-6, SV-845 (30)

Princes Boris and Gleb, sons of Vladimir I, were murdered by their brother in 1015. They were canonized in 1071. Crosses and sheathed swords, referring to their innocent deaths, are their usual attributes.

This icon, given by Boris Godunov, is from the Local tier of the iconostasis of the Cathedral of the Mother of God of Smolensk in the Novodevichy Convent in Moscow.

CAT. NO. 34

CAT. NO. 36

36. ICON OF THE SAVIOR IN GLORY,
late 16th-early 17th century
Moscow
Wood, gesso, tempera, silver gilt,
engraving
214 x 147 x 4
Illustrated on page 56
GIM 103803, NDM 6078/1496/39, SV-852 (1)

From the Deesis tier of the iconosta-
sis of the Cathedral of the Mother of
God of Smolensk in the Novodevichy
Convent in Moscow.

37. ICON OF THE APOSTLE PETER,
late 16th-early 17th century
Moscow
Wood, gesso, tempera, silver gilt
214 x 77 x 3.5
GIM 103803, NDM 6078/1496/36, SV-851 (2)

From the Deesis tier of the iconostasis
of the Cathedral of the Mother of God
of Smolensk in the Novodevichy
Convent in Moscow.

38. ICON OF THE ARCHANGEL MICHAEL,
late 16th-early 17th century
Moscow
Wood, gesso, tempera, silver gilt
214 x 86 x 4
GIM 103803, NDM 6078/1496/37, SV-851 (4)

From the Deesis tier of the iconosta-
sis of the Cathedral of the Mother of
God of Smolensk in the Novodevichy
Convent in Moscow.

39. ICON OF THE ARCHANGEL GABRIEL,
late 16th-early 17th century
Moscow
Wood, gesso, tempera, silver gilt
214 x 87 x 3.5
GIM 103803, NDM 6078/1496/41, SV-851 (5)

From the Deesis tier of the iconostasis
of the Cathedral of the Mother of God
of Smolensk in the Novodevichy
Convent in Moscow.

40. ICON OF THE MOTHER OF GOD,
late 16th-early 17th century
Moscow
Wood, gesso, tempera, silver gilt,
engraving
214 x 76 x 4
GIM 103803, NDM 6078/1486/38, SV-851 (6)

From the Deesis tier of the iconostasis
of the Cathedral of the Mother of God
of Smolensk in the Novodevichy
Convent in Moscow.

41. ICON OF THE APOSTLE PAUL,
late 16th-early 17th century
Moscow
Wood, gesso, tempera, silver gilt
214 x 77 x 4
GIM 103803, NDM 6078/1496/42, SV-851 (7)

From the Deesis tier of the iconostasis
of the Cathedral of the Mother of God
of Smolensk in the Novodevichy
Convent in Moscow.

42. ICON OF THE NATIVITY OF THE
MOTHER OF GOD, late 16th-early
17th century
Moscow
Wood, gesso, tempera, silver gilt
108 x 78 x 3.5
GIM 103803, NDM 6078/1496/15, SV-850 (8)

From the Festival tier of the iconosta-
sis of the Cathedral of the Mother of
God of Smolensk in the Novodevichy
Convent in Moscow.

43. ICON OF THE ENTRY INTO JERUSALEM,
late 16th-early 17th century
Moscow
Wood, gesso, tempera, silver gilt
108 x 78 x 3.5
Illustrated on page 26
GIM 103803, NDM 6078/1496/22, SV-850 (9)

From the Festival tier of the iconostasis
of the Cathedral of the Mother of God
of Smolensk in the Novodevichy
Convent in Moscow.

44. ICON OF THE NATIVITY OF CHRIST,
late 16th-early 17th century
Moscow
Wood, gesso, tempera, silver gilt
108 x 78 x 3.5
Illustrated on page 57
GIM 103803, NDM 6078/1496/20, SV-850 (10)

From the Festival tier of the iconostasis
of the Cathedral of the Mother of God
of Smolensk in the Novodevichy
Convent in Moscow.

45. ICON OF THE BAPTISM OF CHRIST,
late 16th-early 17th century
Moscow
Wood, gesso, tempera, silver gilt
108 x 78 x 3.5
GIM 103803, NDM 6078/1496/21, SV-850 (11)

From the Festival tier of the iconostasis
of the Cathedral of the Mother of God
of Smolensk in the Novodevichy
Convent in Moscow.

CAT. NO. 44

46. ICON OF THE CRUCIFIXION, late 16th-early 17th century
Moscow
Wood, gesso, tempera, silver gilt
108 x 78 x 3.5
Illustrated on page 26
GIM 103803, NDM 6078/1496/24, SV-850 (12)

From the Festival tier of the iconostasis of the Cathedral of the Mother of God of Smolensk in the Novodevichy Convent in Moscow.

47. ICON OF THE ENTOMBMENT, late 16th-early 17th century
Moscow
Wood, gesso, tempera, silver gilt
108 x 78 x 3.5
GIM 103803, NDM 6078/1496/23, SV-850 (13)

From the Festival tier of the iconostasis of the Cathedral of the Mother of God of Smolensk in the Novodevichy Convent in Moscow.

48. ICON OF THE RAISING OF LAZARUS, late 16th-early 17th century
Moscow
Wood, gesso, tempera, silver gilt
108 x 78 x 3.5
GIM 103803, NDM 6078/1496/26, SV-850 (14)

From the Festival tier of the iconostasis of the Cathedral of the Mother of God of Smolensk in the Novodevichy Convent in Moscow.

49. ICON OF THE MOTHER OF GOD OF THE INCARNATION, late 16th-early 17th century
Moscow
Wood, gesso, tempera, silver gilt
155 x 120 x 4
GIM 103803, NDM 6078/1486/57, SV-853 (15)

From the Prophets tier of the iconostasis of the Cathedral of the Mother of God of Smolensk in the Novodevichy Convent in Moscow.

50. ICON OF THE PROPHET MOSES, late 16th-early 17th century
Moscow
Wood, gesso, tempera, silver gilt
155 x 72 x 3.5
GIM 103803, NDM 6078/1496/55, SV-853 (16)

From the Prophets tier of the iconostasis of the Cathedral of the Mother of God of Smolensk in the Novodevichy Convent in Moscow.

51. ICON OF THE PROPHET AARON, late 16th-early 17th century
Moscow
Wood, gesso, tempera, silver gilt
155 x 72 x 3.5
GIM 103803, NDM 6078/1496/59, SV-853 (17)

From the Prophets tier of the iconostasis of the Cathedral of the Mother of God of Smolensk in the Novodevichy Convent in Moscow.

52. ICON OF THE PROPHET SOLOMON, late 16th-early 17th century
Moscow
Wood, gesso, tempera, silver gilt
154 x 69 x 3.5
GIM 103803, NDM 6078/1496/58, SV-853 (18)

From the Prophets tier of the iconostasis of the Cathedral of the Mother of God of Smolensk in the Novodevichy Convent in Moscow.

53. ICON OF THE PROPHET DAVID, late 16th-early 17th century
Moscow
Wood, gesso, tempera, silver gilt
154 x 73 x 3.5
GIM 103803, NDM 6078/1496/56, SV-853 (19)

From the Prophets tier of the iconostasis of the Cathedral of the Mother of God of Smolensk in the Novodevichy Convent in Moscow.

54. ICON OF THE PROPHET DANIEL, late 16th-early 17th century
Moscow
Wood, gesso, tempera, silver gilt
154 x 73 x 3.5
GIM 103803, NDM 6078/1496/52, SV-853 (20)

From the Prophets tier of the iconostasis of the Cathedral of the Mother of God of Smolensk in the Novodevichy Convent in Moscow.

55. ICON OF THE PROPHET ELIJAH, late 16th-early 17th century
Moscow
Wood, gesso, tempera, silver gilt
154 x 70 x 4
GIM 103803, NDM 6078/1496/60, SV-853 (21)

From the Prophets tier of the iconostasis of the Cathedral of the Mother of God of Smolensk in the Novodevichy Convent in Moscow.

56. ICON OF THE NEW TESTAMENT TRINITY, late 16th-early 17th century
Moscow
Wood, gesso, tempera, silver gilt, engraving
245 x 153 x 4
GIM 103803, NDM 6078/1496/73, SV-854 (22)

From the Prophets tier of the iconostasis of the Cathedral of the Mother of God of Smolensk in the Novodevichy Convent in Moscow.

57. ICON OF THE FOREFATHER ADAM, late 16th-early 17th century
Moscow
Wood, gesso, tempera, silver gilt
214 x 78 x 3.5
GIM 103803, NDM 6078/1496/70, SV-854 (23)

From the Forefathers tier of the iconostasis of the Cathedral of the Mother of God of Smolensk in the Novodevichy Convent in Moscow.

58. ICON OF THE FOREFATHER ENOCH, late 16th-early 17th century
Moscow
Wood, gesso, tempera, silver gilt
214 x 78 x 4
GIM 103803, NDM 6078/1496/72, SV-854 (24)

From the Forefathers tier of the iconostasis of the Cathedral of the Mother of God of Smolensk in the Novodevichy Convent in Moscow.

59. ICON OF THE FOREFATHER JOSEPH, late 16th-early 17th century
Moscow
Wood, gesso, tempera, silver gilt
215 x 78 x 4
GIM 103803, NDM 6078/1496/67, SV-854 (25)

From the Forefathers tier of the iconostasis of the Cathedral of the Mother of God of Smolensk in the Novodevichy Convent in Moscow.

60. ICON OF THE FOREFATHER ABEL, late 16th-early 17th century
Moscow
Wood, gesso, tempera, silver gilt
214 x 78 x 4
GIM 103803, NDM 6078/1496/74, SV-854 (26)

From the Forefathers tier of the iconostasis of the Cathedral of the Mother of God of Smolensk in the Novodevichy Convent in Moscow.

61. ICON OF THE FOREFATHER ABRAHAM, late 16th-early 17th century
Moscow
Wood, gesso, tempera, silver gilt
214 x 78 x 3.5
GIM 103803, NDM 6078/1496/75, SV-854 (27)

From the Forefathers tier of the iconostasis of the Cathedral of the Mother of God of Smolensk in the Novodevichy Convent in Moscow.

62. ICON OF THE FOREFATHER ISAAC, late 16th-early 17th century
Moscow
Wood, gesso, tempera, silver gilt
214 x 77 x 3.5
GIM 103803, NDM 6078/1496/76, SV-854 (28)

From the Forefathers tier of the iconostasis of the Cathedral of the Mother of God of Smolensk in the Novodevichy Convent in Moscow.

63. ICON OF THE SMOLENSK MOTHER OF GOD, late 16th-early 17th century
Moscow
Wood, gesso, tempera, silver gilt, chasing, precious stones
104.5 x 78 x 3
GIM 103803, NDM 1252/1318, SV-670 (39)

From the vestry of the Cathedral of the Mother of God of Smolensk in the Novodevichy Convent in Moscow.

64. ICON OF THE VISION OF THE HEAVENLY LADDER (THE VISION OF JOHN LESTVICHNIK), late 16th-early 17th century
Moscow
Wood, gesso, tempera
178 x 140 x 4
GIM 103803, NDM 3311 (43)

From the Cathedral of the Mother of God of Smolensk in the Novodevichy Convent in Moscow.

65. SMALL ICON (PANAGIA) ON A CHAIN, late 16th-early 17th century
Novgorod
Silver, enamel
12.6 x 9.1
GIM 78747, OK 11388 (285)

66. SMALL FOLDING ICON (PANAGIA),
early 17th century
Silver, gilt, carnelian
11 x 4.5
Illustrated on page 60
GIM 3107 shch, OK 7370 (282)

Acquired from the collection of
P. I. Shchukin in 1905.

**67. ICON OF ST. NICHOLAS THE MIRACLE
WORKER,** 17th century
Sculpture in an icon case (kiot)
Wood, paint, carving
106 x 61 x 12
Illustrated on page 33
GIM 78036/1756 (162)

68. ICON OF ST. PARASKEVA PIATNITSA,
17th century
Limewood, pine, paint, carving
71 x 45 x 7
Illustrated on page 60
GIM 24740/1083 (163)

69. ICON OF THE CROSS, 17th century
Carved limewood, tempera
Northern Province
28.4 x 20.2 x 1.8
GIM 2927 shch/260 (178)

**70. DEESIS WITH ICON OF ST. ISAAC,
ST. STEPHEN, AND ST. SERGIUS OF
RADONEZH,** 17th century
Northern Province
Wood, paint, carving
33 x 24 x 2.5
GIM 77958/1079 (185)

CAT. NO. 66

CAT. NO. 68

71. ICON OF ST. NICHOLAS, THE TIKHVIN MOTHER OF GOD, AND ST. PARASKEVA WITH ST. ONUFRY AND ST. MAXIM, 17th century
Wood, tempera, carving
25.3 x 20.6 x 2.2
GIM 78149/293 (187)

72. ICON OF THE SAINTS AND PRINCES VLADIMIR, BORIS, AND GLEB, 17th century
Wood, tempera, carving
23.5 x 21 x 2.5
GIM 70388/1006 (189)

73. FOLDING ICON (SKLADEN) OF THE CRUCIFIXION WITH MOURNERS, DEESIS, AND SAINTS, 17th century
Wood, tempera, silver, carving
10.7 x 29 x 1.8
Illustrated on page 61
GIM 45498/323 (199)

First publication.

74. ICON OF THE CRUCIFIXION, 17th century
Wood, carving
16.5 x 13 x 2
GIM 37130/DU 481 (205)

First publication.

75. PORTABLE ICONOSTASIS (SKLADEN), first half of the 17th century
Cypress, metal, traces of paint, carving
30.5 x 54.5 x 3
GIM 2005 shch/422 (164)

76. FOLDING ICON-SHRINE (SKLADEN), WITH SCENES OF CHRISTIAN FESTIVALS, first half of the 17th century
Possibly Moscow
Wood, silver, gilt, cloth, carving, filigree
16.2 x 11.9
GIM 9203 shch, OK 9173 (280)

The inner sides of the panels depict major Christian religious festivals.
   Acquired from the collection of P. I. Shchukin in 1905.

77. FOLDING ICON (SKLADEN) OF THE MOTHER OF GOD OF KAZAN, first half of the 17th century
Oklad, 1677
Moscow
Wood, tempera, gilt, silver, sapphires, rubies, pearls, niello, casting,
chasing, carving
48.2 x 33.2
GIM 78049, OK 11150 (309)

Acquired from the Anti-Religious Museum of Art in 1935. First Publication.

78. ST. EVDOKIIA, mid-17th century
The Armory Chamber, Moscow
Wood, gesso, tempera, silver, gilding, embossing
45 x 13.5
GIM 103803, NDM 3297/40, SV-799 (34)

This is a *mernaia* or measurement icon of Tsarevna Evdokiia Alexeevna Miloslavskaia.

79. ICON OF THE CROSS, mid-17th century
Northern Province
Limewood, tin, mica, tempera, carving
26 x 21.3 x 2.8
Illustrated on page 30
GIM 36247/874 (177)

CAT. NO. 73

**80. ICONOSTASIS WITH FAMILY ICONS
OF TSAR ALEXIS MIKHAILOVICH,**
mid-17th century
Moscow
Wood, gesso, tempera, mica, pewter
190 x 160 x 10
Illustrated on page 63
GIM 103803, NDM 3317/7, SV-804 (35)

a. THE OLD TESTAMENT TRINITY,
mid-17th century
The Armory Chamber, Moscow
Wood, gesso, tempera, silver,
chasing
111 x 98 x 4
GIM 103803, NDM 3317/2, SV-804

**b. THE INTERCESSION OF THE
MOTHER OF GOD (POKROV),**
late 16th-early 17th century
Wood, gesso, tempera, silver,
chasing
111 x 98 x 4
GIM 103803, NDM 3317/1, SV-804

c. THE METROPOLITAN ALEXIS,
mid-17th century
Wood, gesso, tempera, silver
40 x 31 x 3
GIM 103803, NDM 3317/3, SV-804

**d. THE SLOVENSKAYA MOTHER
OF GOD,** mid-17th century
Wood, gesso, tempera, silver
40 x 33 x 3
GIM 103803, NDM 3317/4, SV-804

**e. THE SLOVENSKAYA MOTHER
OF GOD,** mid-17th century
Wood, gesso, tempera, silver
40 x 33 x 3
GIM 103803, NDM 3317/5, SV-804

**f. THE SLOVENSKAYA MOTHER
OF GOD,** mid-17th century
Wood, gesso, tempera, silver
40 x 33 x 3
GIM 103803, NDM 3317/6, SV-804

**g. THE MAXIMOVSKAIA MOTHER
OF GOD,** mid-17th century
Moscow
Wood, gesso, tempera, silver,
chasing
40 x 31 x 3
GIM 103803, NDM 3317/7, SV-804

This iconostasis was a donation
of Tsar Alexis Mikhailovich to the
Novodevichy Convent in Moscow.
According to tradition, the icons
belonged to his family.

CAT. NO. 80

CAT. NO. 81

81. TWO-SIDED ICON OF THE VLADIMIR MOTHER OF GOD AND THREE METROPOLITANS OF MOSCOW, AND ICON OF ST. PETER, ST. ALEXIS, AND ST. JOHN, mid-17th century
Moscow
Wood, gesso, tempera
56.7 x 44.8 (without handle),
h. 117.5 (with handle)
Illustrated on page 64
GIM 58384, I VIII 3474 (135)

This two-sided icon was used in processions.

82. ICON OF THE CRUCIFIXION, mid-17th century
Northern Province
Cypress, traces of paint, carving
25.1 x 12.2 x 1.5
Illustrated on page 65
GIM 2096 shch/807 (179)

83. ICON OF THE NATIVITY OF THE MOTHER OF GOD, mid-17th century
Yaroslavl
Wood, tempera, silver, gilt, chasing
32.4 x 28
GIM 54627, OK 8013 (307)

The silver chasing in the oklad of this icon is typical of the style of the Yaroslavl School. It is distinctive in its abundant ornamentation and high relief, and it is related to the wood carving for which cities along the Volga River were famous.

CAT. NO. 82

CAT. NO. 84

84. Icon of the Mother of God, Life-Giving Spring, 1670
S. Rozhkov, S. Ushakov
The Armory Chamber, Moscow
Wood, gesso, tempera, silver gilt, chasing, enamel, molding, precious stones, gold
53.5 x 42.5 x 3.5
Illustrated on page 66
GIM 103803, NDM 1309, ZV-60 (37)

Donated by the boyar B. M. Khitrovo to the Novodevichy Convent in Moscow.

85. Icon of the Seventh Ecumenical Council, 1670s
S. Ushakov
The Armory Chamber, Moscow
Wood, gesso, tempera.
175 x 133 x 4
Illustrated on page 29
GIM 103803, NDM 1297/1292 (42)

In 787, the seventh session of the Second Council of Nicaea, also called the Seventh Ecumenical Council, affirmed the veneration of images.

From the Cathedral of the Mother of God of Smolensk in the Novodevichy Convent in Moscow.

86. Icon of Alexis, Man of God,
second half of the 17th century
The Armory Chamber, Moscow
Wood, gesso, tempera
143 x 51.8
GIM 108817, I VIII 5858 (136)

87. Icon of St. Nicholas the Miracle Worker with Scenes from His Life, second half of the 17th century
Carved wood, paint, tin, mica
42 x 34.5 x 6.2
Illustrated on page 67
GIM 39497/1016 (186)

88. Small Icon (Panagia) in the Shape of a Flower with an Image of Christ Blessing, second half of the 17th century
The Armory Chamber, Moscow
Gold, silver, diamonds, enamel, pearls, chasing, carving
8.8 x 6.7
Illustrated on page 38
GIM 77663, OK 9963 (284)

This panagia, in the form of a flower, has a chased and enameled image of the Savior in the center. The choice of stones, their mounting and color, are typical of jewelry styles of the period, especially in the use of lace-work. The panagia demonstrates the influence of Oriental art on Russian gold and silver jewelry of the second half of the 17th century. Both royal and ecclesiastical courts purchased works from Constantinople, which influenced the outstanding quality of Russian church art.

89. Icon of John the Baptist, second half of 17th century
The Armory Chamber, Moscow
Wood, tempera, stones, silver, cloth, glass, enamel, hand stamping, carving, gilt
25.5 x 20.6
GIM 16152, OK 8044 (302)

This delicate and expressive depiction of John the Baptist is enhanced with an oklad of imitation pearls. This style of decoration was widely used by jewelers in Moscow in the second half of the 17th century for creating both sacred and secular objects.

CAT. NO. 87

CAT. NO. 90

90. ICON OF THE SAVIOR IN GLORY,
second half of the 17th century
Yaroslavl
Wood, tempera, silver, gilt, chasing
39.4 x 38.3
Illustrated on page 68
GIM 76322, OK 9184 (310)

91. ICON OF THE CRUCIFIXION WITH
MOURNERS, 1678
L. Stefanov
The Armory Chamber, Moscow
Wood, gesso, tempera, silver gilt,
engraving
54 x 42 x 3.5
Illustrated on page 69
GIM 103803, NDM 1315/1455, SV-675 (38)

Donated by the boyar B. M. Khitrovo
to the Novodevichy Convent in
Moscow.

92. ICON OF ST. PROKOPY AND ST. IOANN,
THE WONDERWORKERS OF USTIUG,
1679
Veliky Ustiug
Wood, tempera, silver, gilt, enamel,
carving, casting, filigree
35 x 30
GIM 57520, OK 13367 (305)

Along with the more common and
widely venerated Christian saints of
the Russian Orthodox Church, local
saints also enjoyed special veneration in some areas of Russia. Two
of these figures, Prokopy (d. 1303)
and Ioann (d. 1494), known as "holy
fools," are depicted in this icon.
Prokopy, born into a wealthy Catholic
family in northwestern Europe, came
to Novgorod, where he converted to
the Orthodox faith and became a
monk. He denounced the life of sin
in the streets of Veliky Ustiug and
was known for his many miracles
and good deeds. Both Prokopy and
Ioann were considered to be patron
saints of Veliky Ustiug, and this icon
was commissioned by a resident of
that town.

CAT. NO. 91

CAT. NO. 93

93. ICON OF SAINTS WITH THE SAME NAME AS TSAR ALEXIS MIKHAILOVICH, 1660s
Fedor Zubov
The Armory Chamber, Moscow
Oklad, 1683 by P. Afanas'ev and N. Pshenichnyi
Wood, gesso, tempera, silver, gilt, engraving, embossing
162 x 126.5 x 5.5
Illustrated on page 70
GIM 103803, NDM 6078/1496/12, SV-849 (31)

Donated by Tsar Alexis Mikhailovich, this icon is from the Local tier of the iconostasis of the Cathedral of the Mother of God of Smolensk in the Novodevichy Convent in Moscow.

94. ICON OF FAITH, HOPE, LOVE, AND THEIR MOTHER SOPHIA, 1685
Karp Zolotarev
The Armory Chamber, Moscow
Wood, gesso, tempera
115 x 73 x 3
Illustrated on page 29
GIM 103803, NDM 1881 (44)

Karp Zolotarev was commissioned by the Tsarevna Sophia to paint this icon for the St. Sophia side chapel in the Cathedral of the Mother of God of Smolensk in the Novodevichy Convent in Moscow.

95. FOLDING ICON-SHRINE (SKLADEN) WITH SCENES OF "THE SAVIOR NOT MADE WITH HANDS," THE MOTHER OF GOD, THE ANNUNCIATION, AND SAINTS, 1691-92
The Armory Chamber, Moscow
Wood, tempera, silver, gilt, pearls, enamel, carving, chasing
25.2 x 10.7 x 3.2
GIM 1701 shch, OK 4178 (281)

A miniature icon of the Mother of God is shown in the central part of the skladen. At the top is the icon of "The Savior Not Made with Hands" and on the side panels are depictions of the Annunciation and saints that were particularly venerated in Moscow.

Acquired from the collection of P. I. Shchukin in 1905.

96. ICON OF THE OLD TESTAMENT TRINITY, last quarter of the 17th century
The Armory Chamber, Moscow
Wood, gesso, tempera, silver, gilt, precious stones, gold, embossing
33 x 27
Illustrated on page 71
GIM 103803, NDM 3287/11, ZV-120 (33)

This icon was a personal possession of Tsarevna Sophia Alexeevna.

97. ICON OF THE PIOUS JOB WITH SCENES FROM HIS LIFE, late 17th century
Moscow
Wood, gesso, gilt, silver gilt, engraving, precious stones
32 x 27 x 3
GIM 103803, NDM 861/793, SV-632 (36)

From the nun's cell of Tsarevna Evdokiia Alexeevna Miloslavsky in the Novodevichy Convent in Moscow.

98. ICON OF ST. ALEXIS, late 17th century
The Armory Chamber, Moscow
Wood, gesso, tempera
144.5 x 69.5 x 3.5
GIM 103803, NDM 2787 (46)

From the Savior's Transfiguration Church in the village of Bolshie Viazemy.

99. ICON OF ST. GEORGE, late 17th century
Wood, tempera, carving
26.1 x 22.3 x 3
GIM 34607/286 (183)

CAT. NO. 96

100. ICON OF THE PANTOCRATOR,
late 17th century
The Armory Chamber, Moscow
Wood, tempera, cloth, gold, silver,
diamonds, sapphires, emeralds,
rubies, pearls, enamel, chasing,
casting, carving
151 x 112.5
Illustrated on page 73
GIM 68889, OK 6202 (308)

101. ICON OF THE MIRACLE OF
ST. GEORGE AND THE DRAGON,
late 17th-early 18th century
Northern Province
Wood, gesso, tempera
106.5 x 91.8
GIM 106405, I VIII 6260 (137)

102. THE INTERCESSION OF THE
MOTHER OF GOD, late 17th-
early 18th century
Wood, tempera
170 x 160
Illustrated on page 25
GIM 103794/531 (108)

First publication.

103. ICON OF ST. NICHOLAS, 17th-18th
century
The Armory Chamber, Moscow
Wood, tempera, gesso
167 x 81 x 4
GIM 103803, NDM 1303/1293 (45)

First publication.

104. ICON OF THE MIRACLE OF
ST. GEORGE AND THE DRAGON,
early 18th century
Northern Province
Wood, gesso, tempera
67.6 x 55
GIM 74139, I VIII 5083 (140)

CAT. NO. 100

CAT. NO. 105

105. ICON OF ST. LEONTY, ST. ANNA,
ST. JOACHIM, AND ST. JUSTINA,
early 18th century
Limewood, tempera, carving
44.5 x 36.6 x 5
Illustrated on page 74
GIM 55298/1025 (188)

106. ICON OF ST. BASIL WITH THE
CATHEDRAL OF THE INTERCESSION
AND THE MOSCOW KREMLIN IN THE
BACKGROUND, 18th century
Moscow
Wood, tempera
141 x 113
Illustrated on page 25
GIM 103974/907 (111)

107. ICON OF THE CROSS AND THE
CRUCIFIXION, 18th century
Wood, tempera, carving
31.5 x 27 x 4.5
GIM 25696/1005 (180)

First publication.

108. DEESIS WITH ICON OF JESUS CHRIST,
THE MOTHER OF GOD, GOD
SABAOTH, AND THE ARCHANGEL,
18th century
Northern Province
Wood, paint, carving
50 x 59 x 10
Illustrated on page 75
44543/940 (184)

109. ICON OF THE BLESSED PRINCE
FEDOR AND HIS SONS DAVID AND
CONSTANTINE WITH ST. BASIL AND
ST. CONSTANTINE, 18th century
Limewood, tempera, carving
18.5 x 17.5 x 2.7
Illustrated on page 75
GIM 77956/805 (190)

110. ICON OF THE DORMITION OF THE
MOTHER OF GOD, 18th century
Wood, tempera, carving
41.2 x 53 x 3.7
Illustrated on page 33
GIM 55639/1034 (192)

111. ICON OF THE LAST JUDGMENT,
18th century
Wood, gesso, tempera
205 x 163 x 3.5
Illustrated on page 26
GIM 103803, NDM 2778 (41)

First publication.

Cat. no. 108

Cat. no. 109

CAT. NO. 113

CAT. NO. 115

112. ICON OF THE MOTHER OF GOD OF THE BURNING BUSH, first half of the 18th century
Cypress, carving
29 x 22.2 x 2.3
GIM 22248 shch/922 (193)

First publication.

113. ICON OF FESTIVALS AND SAINTS, 1752
Elisha Zayats
Cypress, carving
38.3 x 20.4 x 1
Illustrated on page 76
GIM 23857/974 (194)

114. ICON OF THE MOTHER OF GOD OF VATOPED, 1752
Andrey Gerasimov
Moscow
Wood, tempera, silver, gilt, chasing
51.7 x 39.5
GIM 77361, OK 10628 (313)

Acquired from the Anti-Religious Museum in 1935.

115. ICON OF THE CRUCIFIXION WITH MOURNERS, 1775
Alexey Solovetsky, The Solovetsky Monastery
Wood, tempera, carving
95 x 68.5 x 3
Illustrated on page 76
GIM 20911 shch/1656 (195)

This icon was commissioned by the merchant Elijha Emelianov from Olonetsk.

116. ICON OF ST. PAPHNUTIUS OF BOROVSK, 1780
Fedor Andreyanov
Moscow
Wood, tempera, silver, gilt, enamel, filigree
33 x 27.7
Illustrated on page 77
GIM 58383/93, OK 8130 (312)

St. Paphnutius of Borovsk (1394-1477) was canonized in 1548, during the time of Ivan the Terrible. The depictions of nature in the oklad of the icon, executed in a technique of enamel on filigree, reminded the viewer of the life and teaching of St. Paphnutius and his search for the spiritual unification of divine and human nature.

117. ICON OF THE MOTHER OF GOD,
"BANISH MY SORROWS," 1790
Moscow
Wood, gesso, tempera
108.5 x 82
Illustrated on page 78
GIM 82847, I VIII 3607 (139)

118. ICON OF THE APOSTLES ST. PETER
AND ST. PAUL, 1796
Moscow
Wood, gesso, tempera
106.2 x 82.5
GIM 108818, I VIII 5353 (138)

119. ICON OF ST. THEODOSIUS OF TOTEM,
late 18th century
Northern Province
Wood, gesso, tempera
83.6 x 53.5
GIM 67591, I VIII 5088 (141)

120. ICON OF ST. NICHOLAS, 1807
Moscow
Wood, tempera, silver, filigree
30.3 x 26.1
GIM 77356, OK 10048 (320)

121 THE OLD TESTAMENT TRINITY,
1812/31
Moscow
Silver, enamel, copper, wood,
casting
50 x 50
GIM 68257/166, OK 9502 (349)

A regimental icon of the Viatsky
Infantry, the inscription reads that
it was made in 1812 and re-worked
in 1831 "in memory of those killed
in 1812, 1828, and 1829."

122. ICON OF CHRIST IN THE DUNGEON,
early 19th century
Moscow
Wood, paint, cloth, carving
125 x 45 x 45
GIM 45296/1443 (159)

From the Church of St. Peter and
St. Paul on Novobasmannaya Street
in Moscow. First publication.

CAT. NO. 116

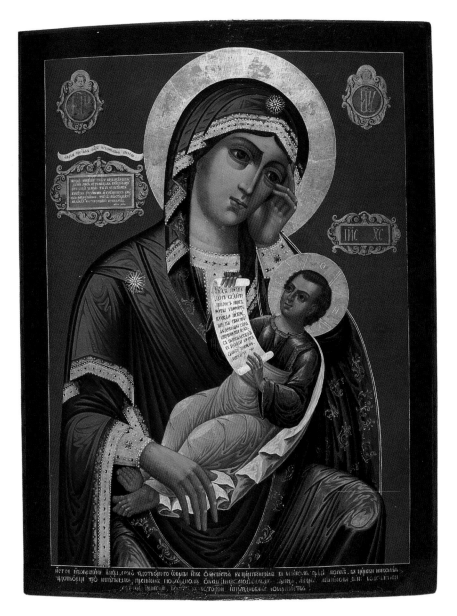

CAT. NO. 117

123. ICON OF JOHN THE THEOLOGIAN,
early 19th century
Moscow
Wood, gilt, paint, carving
132 x 34 x 26
GIM 45296/1432 (160)

Part of a sculptural composition of
the Crucifixion with mourners from
the Church of St. Peter and St. Paul
on Novobasmannaya Street in
Moscow. First publication.

124. ICON OF WOMEN BEARING MYRRH,
early 19th century
Moscow
Wood, gilt, paint, carving
110 x 39 x 19
GIM 45296/1433 (161)

Part of a sculptural composition of
the Crucifixion with mourners from
the Church of St. Peter and St. Paul
on Novobasmannaya Street in
Moscow.

125 ICON OF ST. CYRIL, ST. JOHN,
AND A GUARDIAN ANGEL, early
19th century
Wood, tempera, carving
21.5 x 18.5 x 1.8
GIM 2849 shch/803 (191)

First publication.

126. ICON OF NICHOLAS RADOVITSKY,
1840
Ryazan Province
Wood, birch bark, stamping,
engraving, carving
46.8 x 39 x 4
GIM 72081/1181 (196)

First publication.

127. ICON OF THE MOTHER OF GOD OF
TENDERNESS, 1908-17
Moscow
Oklad, P. I. Olovianishnikov & Sons
Wood, tempera, silver, enamel,
filigree
31 x 27
GIM 103173/16, OK 18346 (354)

78

CAT. NO. 128

**128. FOLDING ICON (SKLADEN) WITH
THE OLD TESTAMENT TRINITY,
THE MOTHER OF GOD, AND
ST. NICHOLAS, 1915**
Moscow
Silver, wood, enamel, gilt
78.5 x 59 (open)
Illustrated on page 79
GIM 103173/19, OK 21123 (357)

On the back, the inscription reads:
"To priest Alexander Kuvakin,
deeply respected pastor, Prior of
the Trinity Church in the village
of Karacharovo, on the occasion
of the 25th anniversary of his
pastorship in this church from
grateful and loving parishioners.
27.XI.1890-27.XI.1915."

CAT. NO. 129

129. ROYAL DOORS WITH THE ANNUNCIATION, ST. JOHN CHRYSOSTOM, AND ST. BASIL THE GREAT, late 15th-early 16th century
Novgorod
Wood, gesso, tempera
141.3 x 37 (left door),
141.3 x 37.4 (right door)
Illustrated on page 80
GIM 55053, I VIII 4832 (124)

The Royal Doors are the central doors of an iconostasis.

130. ALTAR CROSS, 16th century
Novgorod
Wood, silver, gilt, casting, hand stamping
44.5 x 21.8
GIM 58383, OK 14017 (278)

Crosses like this are an integral part of altar decoration. The casting of the Crucifixion with mourners on one side of this cross is typical of Novgorodian style of small-scale, three dimensional art of the 15th and 16th centuries. Noteworthy is the extremely complex ornamentation with volutes, spirals, and rosettes.
     Acquired from the Rumiantsev Museum (Zubalov Collection) in 1923.

131. ICON CASE (KIOT), late 16th century
Wood, tempera, carving
149 x 56 x 36
GIM 42148/1729 (148)

132. CROSS, late 16th century
Cypress, carving
25.6 x 18 x 2
GIM 37826/447 (174)

First publication.

133. CROSS, late 16th-early 17th century
Northern Province
Wood, tempera, carving
24.5 x 14.2 x 1.7
Illustrated on page 30
GIM 74724/476 (173)

134. ROYAL DOORS, 17th century
Yaroslavl Province
Wood, paint, carving
Two panels: 165 x 45.5 x12,
165 x 40 x 6
GIM 17166 shch/1345 a, b (142)

The Royal Doors are the central doors of an iconostasis.

135. WINDOW WITH IMAGE OF THE HOLY GHOST, 17th century
Wood, mica, tin
134 x 84 x 3.5
GIM 20778/1571 (151)

136. CANDLESTICK, 17th century
Wood, paint, grooving
H. 120, diam. 23
GIM 36263/1498 (153)

137-142. SIX FIGURES FROM A DEESIS, 17th century
Northern Province
Wood, paint, carving
Illustrated on page 32

THE MOTHER OF GOD
52 x 13 x 1.5
GIM 42667/302 (165)

JOHN THE BAPTIST
52 x 12 x 1.5
GIM 42668/303 (166)

THE ARCHANGEL GABRIEL
52 x 13 x 1.5
GIM 42669/304 (167)

THE ARCHANGEL MICHAEL
52.5 x 15.5 x 1.5
GIM 42670/305 (168)

THE APOSTLE PAUL
52.5 x 14 x 1.5
GIM 42671/306 (169)

THE APOSTLE PETER
53 x 13.5 x 1.5
GIM 42672/307 (170)

143. CROSS, 17th century
Wood, tempera, metal, carving
20 x 10.3 x 2.3
GIM 4672 shch/18 (175)

First publication.

144. TABLE, 17th century
Moscow
Wood, tempera
73 x 114 x 59
GIM 19234/DU 665 (201)

From the chambers of Tsarevna
Sophia in the Novodevichy Convent.

145. MONASTERY ARMCHAIR, 17th century
Wood, carving
81 x 52 x 41
GIM 4333 shch/DU1355 (202)

146. ICON CASE (KIOT), 17th century
Wood, paint, carving
38 x 36 x 5
GIM 22256/DU 1183 (204)

First publication.

147. PART OF A DEESIS, second half
of the 17th century
Wood, paint, carving
19 x 40 x 2.5
Illustrated on page 81
GIM 16453 shch/987 (171)

148. CANDLESTICK, 1655
Wood, tempera, tin, copper, iron,
cloth
65 x 24 x 24
Illustrated on page 81
GIM 40574/1501 (152)

**149. LITURGICAL PLATE WITH
ALLEGORIES OF THE SEASONS,**
second half of the 17th century
Wood, tempera, carving
H. 10, diam. 63
GIM 2122 shch/1531 (150)

CAT. NO. 147

CAT. NO. 148

CAT. NO. 151

150. ROYAL DOORS, 1685
Stepan Zinov'ev
Moscow
Wood, gesso, gilt, carving
200 x 70 x 16
GIM 103803, NDM 6078/1, SV-843 (29)

Six medallions:

a. MOTHER OF GOD
Metal, tempera, silver gilt
30 x 25

b. THE ARCHANGEL GABRIEL
Metal, tempera, silver gilt
30 x 25

c. MATTHEW THE EVANGELIST
Metal, tempera, silver gilt
30 x 25

d. MARK THE EVANGELIST
Metal, tempera, silver gilt
30 x 25

e. LUKE THE EVANGELIST
Metal, tempera, silver gilt
30 x 25

f. JOHN THE EVANGELIST
Metal, tempera, silver gilt
30 x 25

**151. PROCESSIONAL CROSS, late 17th
century**
Wood, tempera, carving
111 x 62 x 3
Illustrated on page 82
GIM 44647/1325 (149)

First publication.

152. CROSS, late 17th century
Limewood, tempera, gilt, carving
72.5 x 40.7
GIM 26792/1013 (172)

153. CANDLESTICK, late 17th century
Wood, paint, carving
131 x 24.5
GIM 17293 shch/1239 (203)
First publication.

**154. LECTERN, late 17th-early 18th
century**
Wood, carving, paint, leather
123 x 55 x 42
GIM 17152 shch/1293 (156)

155. CROSS, late 17th-early 18th century
Wood, paint, metal, carving
23.6 x 15 x 2.2
GIM 29999/3 (176)

First publication.

156. ALTAR CROSS, 1720
Moscow
Wood, silver
20 x 10.5
GIM 103801/8 (116)

An inscription on the grip states
that the cross was given to the
Chapel of the Nativity of the Virgin
in the Cathedral of the Intercession
(St. Basil's). First publication.

157. ALTAR CROSS, 1726
Moscow
Wood, silver
33 x 18
GIM 103801/7 (115)

An inscription on the grip states
that the cross was given to the
Chapel of the Nativity of the Virgin
in the Cathedral of the Intercession
(St. Basil's). First publication.

158. BISHOP'S CHAIR, mid-18th century
Wood, paint, gilt, velvet, carving
171 x 87 x 57
GIM 77248/905 (157)

**159. ROYAL DOORS WITH A CANOPY AND
PAINTING OF THE ANNUNCIATION,**
second half of the 18th century
Central Russia
Wood, gilt, paint, carving
Doors: 130 x 70 x 14
Canopy: 88 x 114 x 14
GIM 866841/1677, 86842/1678, 86843/1679 (143)

160. ROYAL DOORS, second half of
the 18th century
Wood, gilt, tempera
Two panels: 253 x 66 x 9.5,
260 x 60.5 x 4
GIM 21455/1371 (144)

First publication.

**161. ROYAL DOORS WITH A PAINTING
OF THE LAST SUPPER,** second half
of the 18th century
Wood, gilt, paint, carving
Two panels: 153 x 53 x 12,
153 x 46 x7
GIM 39894/1362 (145)

162. ROYAL DOORS, second half of
the 18th century
Wood, gilt, tempera, carving
Two panels: 176 x 55 x 8,
175 x 42 x 4.5
GIM 17168 shch/1358 (146)

First publication.

163-164. PAIR OF CANDLESTICKS, 1915
Wood, paint, metal
H. 117, diam. 32 (each)
GIM 54679/1648, 54679/1649 (154-155)

First publication.

**165. CROSS WITH SCENE OF THE
CRUCIFIXION,** early 20th century
S. Vashkov
P. I. Olovianishnikov & Sons,
Moscow
Wood, tempera, carving
210 x 125 x 35
GIM 36972/1687 (158)

CAT. NO. 166

CAT. NO. 167

166. LITURGICAL PLATE, 16th century
Silver, engraving
Diam. 27
Illustrated on page 84
GIM 103805, NDM 1337/332, SB-203 (85)

The inscription on the rim reads: "The plate of the Grand Prince, a son of the Grand Prince Yury Ivanovich. This liturgical plate in the memory of Princess Alexandra Oudelelina [sic]."

Donated by Uliana Udelina to the Novodevichy Convent in Moscow.

167. PECTORAL CROSS WITH THE CRUCIFIXION, FRONT, AND ST. NICHOLAS THE MIRACLE WORKER, BACK, 16th century
Novgorod
Gold, silver, sapphires, tourmalines, pearls, chasing, carving
11.5 x 6
Illustrated on page 84
GIM 77661, OK 9962 (277)

Only priests and tsars could wear a richly decorated cross on a chain outside their clothes, but all members of the Orthodox Church could wear a pectoral cross (tel'nic) under their clothes.

Acquired from the Northern Museum of Regional Studies in 1935.

168. BASIN FOR HOLY WATER, 1581
Silver, gilt, chasing
H. 25, diam. 38
Illustrated on page 22
GIM 103805, NDM 3284/300, SV-426 (78)

The inscription on the bowl reads: "In the Summer of 7090 [1581] in the month of December on the fifteenth day by the order of Tsarevich Prince Ivan Ivanovich this basin was made for the Oten Hermitage of the Novodevichy Convent for the Church of the Holiest Mother of God Hodegitria."

Donated by Tsar Ivan the Terrible to the Novodevichy Convent in Moscow.

169. CENSER, 1597
Moscow
Silver, gilt, casting, carving
H. 33.5
Illustrated on page 37
GIM 19520, OK 6905 (291)

This censer is a very rare example of the gold and silver jewelry of medieval Russia. The cover resembles the peaked roof of an Orthodox church and its miniature images are of God Enthroned and the saints of the Deesis. The inscription on the lower part of the censer reads that it was manufactured under the reign of Tsar Fedor Ivanovich (1584-98) by the order of Archimandrite Sergius of the Spaso-Prebrazhensky Stone Monastery. The monastery, one of the oldest in northern Russia, was located on an island in Lake Kubenskoe. Legend says that it was founded around 1260 by Prince Gleb Vasilkovich, the first prince of the independent White Lake Principality. After it closed at the end of the 18th century, its valuable works of art were dispersed.

170. CHALICE (POTIR), late 16th-early 17th century
Bowl made in Moscow, stem and base probably made in Italy
Silver, gilt, enamel, glass, casting, carving, chasing
H. 25, diam. 15
Illustrated on page 85
GIM 68945, OK 6172 (292)

The style of the carved image of the Deesis, the Cross of Golgotha, and the liturgical inscriptions relate this chalice to the work of Moscow jewelers working during the reign of Boris Godunov (1598-1605). The ornamentation on the middle and lower parts of the chalice indicated they were probably made in Italy.

171. CENSER, 17th century
Russia
Silver, gilt, chasing, engraving
H. 26
GIM 103805, NDM 1314/344, SV-674 (82)

The inscription on the lower edge reads: "This censer was given to the Tsarevna for Christmas by Stefanida Semenovna Morozova, the widow of the boyar." A second inscription on the bottom reads: "This censer was given by an old man, Ijasaph, to the Intercession Monastery of the Holiest Mother of God his Guardian."

Donated by the boyar Stefanida Morozova.

172. VOTIVE LAMP (LAMPADA),
17th century
Silver, carving, chasing
12.1 x 12 x 12
GIM 49622, OK 8731 (317)

The body is pierced with strapwork of large flowers incorporating the crown of the Grand Prince and religious subjects.

173. ALTAR CROSS, 17th century
Moscow
Silver, gilt, rubies, emeralds, niello, casting
21.5 x 39
GIM 67739, OK 7050 (318)

On the back of the cross is a cast representation of the Crucifixion with mourners.

Acquired from the State Repository of Valuables (Vishnevsky Collection) in 1929.

174. CHALICE (POTIR), 1638
Moscow
Silver, engraving
H. 14, diam. 21
GIM 103801/17 (119)

The inscription on the stem of the chalice describes the commission of the chalice by Tsar Mikhail Fedorovich for the Cathedral of the Intercession (St. Basil's).

175. BASIN FOR HOLY WATER, 1642
Moscow
Silver, gilt, plaster, carving, chasing, casting
H. 37, diam. 43.5
GIM 1000 shch, OK 8041 (296)

The inscription on the rim of the basin reads that it was donated to the John the Baptist Monastery in Tula by Ulyana Golovina, a noble Russian woman, in memory of her deceased relatives.

Acquired from the collection of P. I. Shchukin in 1905.

176. CHALICE (POTIR), 1654
Tobolsk
Silver, gilt, chasing, carving
24.8 x 14.8 x 14.8
GIM 1532 shch, OK 6495 (293)

The inscription on the chalice reads that it was made for the Church of the Appearance of the Mother of God to the Holy Mother of God of Vladimir in Tobolsk. This is a rare example made in Siberia during the time of Patriarch Nikon (1605-1681), who played a significant role in church and state history.

Acquired from the collection of P. I. Shchukin in 1905.

177. LITURGICAL SPOON (LZHITSA),
1661-62
Moscow
Silver, gilt, casting
L. 22.3
GIM 78785, OK 11241 (289)

Acquired from the State Depository of Valuables in 1937.

178. CHURCH KNIFE (KOPIE), second half of 17th century
Silver, gilt, casting, carving
L. 15.2
GIM 1666 shch, OK 6617 (290)

Acquired from the collection of P. I. Shchukin in 1905.

CAT. NO. 170

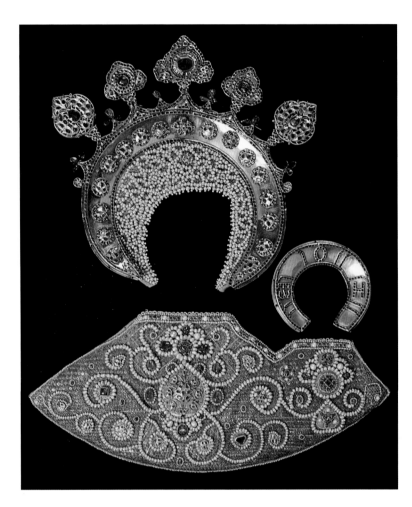

CAT. NO. 179

179. DECORATION FOR THE ICON OF THE MOTHER OF GOD OF SMOLENSK,
second half of the 17th century
The Armory Chamber, Moscow
Gold, silver, diamonds, rubies, emeralds, sapphires, pearls, cloth, enamel, casting, chasing
Illustrated on page 86
GIM 54354, OK 1200/1-4 (311)

   a. CROWN FOR THE MOTHER OF GOD
   34.5 x 38

   b. CROWN FOR CHRIST
   12.8 x 14

   c. SCARF
   21. 5 x 23

   d. NECKLACE
   23 x 53

According to tradition, these decorations were donated by the boyar Bogdan Matveevich Khitrovo (1615/16-1680), an important figure in Russian history.

Acquired from the Intercession Church of the village of Bratsevo in 1923.

180. CENSER, 1677
Yaroslavl
Silver, gilt, chasing, carving
H. 30.8
GIM 4392 shch, OK 6901 (294)

An inscription states that this censer was made under the auspices of Father Superior Selivester of the Afansaiev Monastery, which was founded in Yaroslavl in the 16th century. In 1658 both the buildings and possessions of the monastery were destroyed by fire. The monastery was rebuilt, and this censer, dated 1677, was one of the items that was replaced.

Acquired from the collection of P. I. Shchukin in 1905.

181. ALTAR CROSS, 1679
The Armory Chamber, Moscow
Silver, niello
36.5 x 20.2
GIM 80253, OK 12379 (285)

According to an inscription on the
handle, this cross was made during
the reign of Tsar Fedor Alexeevich
Romanov and was to be donated
to a church in the Kremlin.

182. BASIN FOR HOLY WATER, 1685
Moscow
Copper, chasing, painting
H. 114, diam. 112
GIM 103806, NDM 3324 (88)

From the Novodevichy Convent
in Moscow.

183. VOTIVE LAMP (KANDILO), 1685
Moscow
Silver, gilt, chasing
Diam. 38
GIM 103805, NDM 2994/226, SB-280 (100)

184. VOTIVE LAMP (KANDILO), 1685
Moscow
Silver, gilt, carving
Diam. 38
GIM 103805, NDM 2993/227, SB-279 (101)

185. VOTIVE LAMP (KANDILO), 1685
Moscow
Silver, gilt, carving
Diam. 38
GIM 103805, NDM 3176/161, SB-325 (104)

186. VOTIVE LAMP (KANDILO), 1686
Ivan Yakovlev
Moscow
Silver, gilt, engraving, niello
Diam. 39
Illustrated on page 87
GIM 103805, NDM 1319/314, SB-194 (81)

The inscription in the cartouches
reads: "In the Year 7194 [1686] on
the 6th of November by the order
of Great Sovereigns and Grand
Princes Ioann [Ivan V] Alexeevich,
Peter Alexeevich [Peter I], and Great
Sovereign Blessed Tsarevna and
Grand Princess Sophia Alexeevna of
All Russia and Maly and Bely Russia
Autocrats, this lamp was built for
the Novodevichy Convent. For the
Cathedral of the Holiest Mistress,
our Mother of God and Virgin Mary
and glorious Hodegitria, the miracle-
working icons of Smolensk."

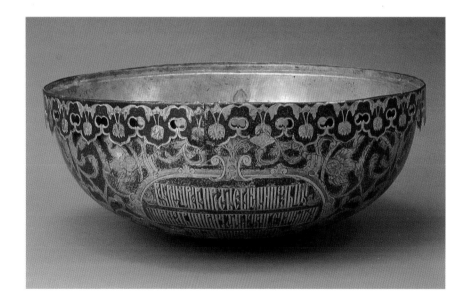

CAT. NO. 186

CAT. NO. 195

187. VOTIVE LAMP (KANDILO), 1686
Ivan Yakovlev
Moscow
Silver, gilt, engraving, niello
Diam. 38
GIM 103805, NDM 1324/343, SB-198 (98)

Donated by Tsars Ivan V and Peter I and Tsarevna Sophia to the Novo-devichy Convent in Moscow.

188. VOTIVE LAMP (KANDILO), 1686
Moscow
Silver, gilt, chasing
Diam. 38
GIM 103805, NDM 3186/340, SB-331 (99)

First publication.

189. VOTIVE LAMP (KANDILO), 1686
Moscow
Silver, gilt, carving
Diam. 37.5
GIM 103805, NDM 1329/342, SB-201 (102)

190. CHALICE (POTIR), 1686
The Armory Chamber, Moscow
Silver, niello
H. 32.5, diam. 16.4
Illustrated on page 39
GIM 99867, OK 16241 (315)

The inscription along the lower edge of the base of this chalice says that it was donated by the boyar Prince Vaily Vasilievich Golitsin (1643-1714) to the Church of the Resurrection of Jesus Christ, and that is was commissioned to give thanks for eternal peace and an end to wars between Russia and Poland.

191. PLATE (DISCOS) WITH AGNUS DEI, 1686
The Armory Chamber, Moscow
Silver, gilt, niello
Diam. 27.5
Illustrated on page 39
GIM 99866, OK 16244 (316)

192. VOTIVE LAMP (KANDILO), 1686
Moscow
Silver, gilt, carving
Diam. 38.5
GIM 103805, NDM 1332/341, SB-202 (103)

193. TABERNACLE, 1686 (1698?)
Russia
Silver gilt, casting, engraving
20 x 13 x 12.5
GIM 103805, NDM 1310/330, SB-190 (80)

The inscription on the bottom edge of the tabernacle reads: "This shrine is built for the House of the Holiest Mother of God of Smolensk in the Novodevichy Convent during the reign of the worthiest Sovereign Tsar and Grand Prince Peter Alexeevich [Peter I], Autocrat of All Great Russia and Maly Russia and Bely Russia by the efforts of Mother Superior Pamphilia and by the good advice of Fevronia in the year of 7206 [1698] of November 26, and it weighs three funts and 68 zolotniks."

Donated by Mother Pamphilia to the Novodevichy Convent in Moscow.

194. LITURGICAL BOWL WITH COVER, 1687
Ivan Yakovlev
Moscow
Silver, gilt, precious stones, niello
H. 15
GIM 103805, NDM 3278/191, ZV-118 (86)

The inscription in the cartouches reads: "By the will of Sovereign pious Tsarevna and Grand Princess Sophia Alexeevna, this bowl was made for the house of her great majesty in the Year 7195 [1687] on the first day of September."

From the Novodevichy Convent in Moscow.

195. CUP WITH COVER, 1687
Ivan Yakovlev
Moscow
Silver, gilt, niello
H. 20, diam. 17
Illustrated on page 88
GIM 103805, NDM 3277/190, SV-350 (87)

The inscription in the cartouches reads: "By the will of Great Sovereign Noble Tsarevna and Grand Princess Sophia Alexeevna, Autocrat of All Russia and Maly Russia and Bely Russia, this cup was made for the house of the Great Sovereign in the Year 7195 [1687]."

From the Novodevichy Convent in Moscow.

196. CHALICE (POTIR), 1692
Russia
Silver, gilt, engraving
H. 26.5
GIM 103805, NDM 1318/327, SB-193 (83)

The inscription on the lower rim reads: "In the year 7200 [1692], this chalice was made for the Novodevichy Convent during the reign of pious Sovereigns and Tsars and Grand Princes Ioann Alexeevich [Ivan V] and Peter Alexeevich [Peter I], Autocrats of all Russia and Maly Russia and Bely Russia, as a donation of the priest and monk Varfalomey to the Cathedral for eternal memory."

197. BASIN FOR HOLY WATER, 1693
The Armory Chamber, Moscow
Silver, gilt, niello, carving
H. 15, diam. 22
Illustrated on page 39
GIM 104606/2, OK 22731 (297)

Considered to be a rare example because of the quality of its decoration, this basin has an inscription saying that it was donated by Archimandrite Varfolomey to the Danilov Trinity Monastery (founded on the outskirts of Vladimir in 1508).

Acquired at an international auction in Switzerland in 1982.

198. ALTAR CROSS, 1694
Moscow
Wood, silver
37 x 21.5
GIM 103801/5 (114)

The grip bears an inscription saying that the cross was given to the Trinity Chapel in the Cathedral of the Intercession (St. Basil's).

199. ALTAR CROSS WITH THE CRUCIFIXION, THE MOTHER OF GOD, AND JOHN THE BAPTIST, 1694
The Armory Chamber, Moscow
Gold, silver, diamonds, emeralds, rubies, pearls, enamel, wood, casting, chasing
38.5 x 20
Illustrated on page 38
GIM 68924, OK 6186 (286)

An inscription on the handle reads that this cross was given by Tsaritsa Natalia Cyrillovna Naryshkina, the mother of Peter the Great, to the Convent of the Assumption, founded in Alexandrov in the 17th century.

Acquired from the Alexandrov City Museum in 1930.

200. CHALICE (POTIR), 1695
Silver, gilt, carving
H. 27.8
GIM 103805, NDM 1327/328, SB-200 (84)

The inscription on the lower rim reads: "In the Year 7203 [1695] on March 18, this church vessel was made for the Transfiguration Church of the Novodevichy Convent."

Donated to the Transfiguration Church of the Novodevichy Convent in Moscow.

201. LITURGICAL VESSEL (DISCOS), WITH THE AGNUS DEI, ANGELS, AND SYMBOLS OF THE EVANGELISTS, 1698
Moscow
Silver, gilt, carving, chasing
H. 11.3, diam. 31
GIM 75049/2, OK 8538 (287)

The image on the plate is that of the Agnus Dei surrounded by angels and the symbols of the Evangelists. The design is enriched with a foliate motif and a "viaz," or ornamental liturgical inscription.

202. PECTORAL CROSS WITH CHAIN, late 17th century
Veliky Ustiug
Silver, enamel, casting, filigree
7.2 x 6.7
GIM 54657/120, OK 5492 (314)

Several artistic centers led the way in the development of liturgical objects in the 17th century. Increasing awareness of the styles of western Europe was also an important influence on the creative imagination of Russian jewelers.

203. LITURGICAL PLATE (ZVEZDITSA OR ASTERISKOS) WITH SAINTS AND THE ADORATION OF THE SHEPHERDS, late 17th century
Moscow
Small plaques (drobnitsa), early 18th century in Vologda
Silver, gilt, niello, carving
H. 11.5
GIM 78724, OK 11234 (288)

This liturgical plate synthesizes the styles of two Russian artistic schools. The portion crafted in Moscow portrays seraphs and selected saints associated with Moscow arranged on a formation of arches. The central plaque (drobnitsa), which is decorated with the rarely represented subject of the Adoration of the Shepherds, as well as other images, reflects the delicate and realistic style of niello which is distinctive of the Vologda masters.

Acquired from the State Depository of Valuables in 1937.

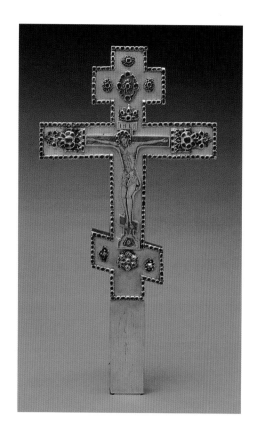

CAT. NO. 204

CAT. NO. 208

204. ALTAR CROSS, 1703
Russia
Gold, silver, precious stones,
engraving
39 x 20
Illustrated on page 90
GIM 103805, NDM 1323/315, ZV-62 (79)

An inscription on the grip of this
cross reads: "This life-giving Cross
is made by efforts of the noble
Sovereign Tsarevna and Grand
Princess nun Susanna Alexeevna
and the noble Sovereign Tsarevna
and Grand Princess Feodosia
Alexeevna for the Hermitage of
the Holiest Mother of God of the
Novodevichy Convent at the time
of the Mother Superior Pamphilia
with the sisters in Christ in the year
from the birth of Jesus Christ 1703
the first day of July."

205. VESSEL FOR THE SACRAMENT (PYX),
1710
Moscow
Silver, gilt, chasing, carving
15 x 10 x. 5.4
GIM 77191, OK 9898 (325)

206. WEDDING CROWN, 1719
Moscow
Silver, gilt, casting, chasing
H. 28
GIM 77633, OK 10838 (333)

Acquired from the Anti-Religious
Museum of Art in 1935.

207. BOWL FOR VOTIVE LAMP, 1722
Silver, carving, casting
8.4 x 22.3 x 22.3
GIM 53080, OK 4203 (334)

The inscription on the rim of the
bowl states that the icon lamp, with
the image of the All-Merciful Savior,
was commissioned by Ivan Ivanov,
son of Rzhevsky. First publication.

208. BASIN FOR HOLY WATER, 1722
Moscow
Silver, gilt, chasing
23.8 x 30.7
Illustrated on page 90
GIM 77251, OK 9913 (335)

The inscription on the base states that the basin was donated to the Church of Cosmos and Damianos in Nizhnii Sadovniki, which was located within the borders of Moscow on the banks of the Moscow River. First publication.

209. LITURGICAL OBJECT (RIPIDION),
early 18th century
Moscow
Silver, carving
17.8 x 14.5
GIM 78901, OK 11385 (324)

As a rule, a six-winged seraph was depicted on the inner surface of a ripidion. The representation of the Annunciation here makes this example a rare deviation from the traditional form of decoration.

Acquired from the State Depository of Valuables in 1937.

210. CROSS, early 18th century
Silver, gold, emeralds, enamel, casting
29.5 x 14.7
GIM 77283, OK 10497 (326)

The cross was used by the priest for blessing the congregation during the liturgy, and it was used to bless the communion bread, wheat, wine, and anointing oil.

Acquired from the Anti-Religious Museum of Art in 1935.

211. CROSS, 18th century
Moscow
Silver, metal
8.5 x 7.7
GIM 103801/43 (118)
First publication.

212. CANDLESTICK, 18th century
Moscow
Silver-plated copper
H. 136
GIM 1033798/60 (120)

First publication.

213. CANDLESTICK, 18th century
Moscow
Silver-plated copper
H. 136
GIM 103798/61(121)

First publication.

214. LITURGICAL OBJECT (PANAGIA),
first quarter of the 18th century
Gold, silver, diamonds, rubies, sapphires, enamel
15 x 7.7
GIM 81556/76, OK 13409 (321)

On one side of the enamel plaque is a representation the Savior in Blessing with cherubs, and on the other is a poorly preserved half-length portrait of Peter the Great. In the first half of the 18th century, it was the custom to bestow panagias with an image of the donor-sovereign upon the higher ranking clergy of the Russian Orthodox Church.

Acquired from the State Depository of Valuables in 1941. First publication.

215. ICON OF THE ANNUNCIATION, 1736
St. Petersburg
Silver, enamel, chasing
18.7 x 13.2
GIM 8948 shch, OK 10840 (319)

Acquired from the collection of P. I. Shchukin in 1905.

216. VOTIVE LAMP (KANDILO), 1751
St. Petersburg
Silver, casting, chasing
38 x 34
GIM 80192/2, OK 12475 (341)

First publication.

217. LITURGICAL OBJECT (PANAGIA),
mid-18th century
Gold, silver, rubies, rosettes, enamel
12 x 7
GIM 81559, OK 13419 (522)

This silver medallion, in the form of a heart, portrays a miniature enamel portrait of the Empress Elizabeth Petrova (ruled 1741-62), daughter of Peter the Great.

Acquired from the State Depository of Valuables in 1941. First publication.

218. LITURGICAL OBJECT (PANAGIA) ON A CHAIN WITH A DEPICTION OF THREE SAINTS
Panagia cast 1761, Moscow
Miniature, 1755 by Michael Lopov, St. Petersburg
Silver, enamel, sapphires, glass
12 x 7.4
GIM 77659, OK 9964 (523)

219. VOTIVE LAMP (LAMPADA) ON A CHAIN, 1770s
Fedor Studentsov
Moscow
Silver, casting, chasing
H. 17, diam. 8
GIM 44644, OK 4199 (337)

CAT. NO. 220

220. CIBORIUM, 1774
Fedor Studentsov
Moscow
Silver, gilt, niello, casting, carving,
chasing
56.3 x 24 x 19.2
Illustrated on page 92
GIM 80107, OK 11867 (331)

Acquired from the Architecture
Museum in 1939.

221. VESPERS VESSEL, 1780s
St. Petersburg
Silver, casting, chasing
30 x 52 x. 35.7
GIM 68257/663, OK 9466 (332)

**222. PART OF AN ICON CASE (KIOT)
FOR THE ICON OF THE MOTHER OF
GOD OF FEDOROV, 1783**
G. S. Ratkov
Kostroma
Silver, gilt, niello, carving, chasing
62.5 x 39
GIM 75519, OK 8664 (342)

The icon of the Mother of God of
Fedorov was a domestic icon of the
first tsars of the Romanov dynasty
and was considered to be a protector of the dynasty. The scenes on
the border of the kiot portray the
miracles associated with this icon.
First publication.

**223. VESSEL FOR THE SACRAMENT (PYX)
WITH "THE SHROUD," 1784**
Russia
Silver, niello, carving, chasing
10.3 x 22.7 x 11
GIM 77234, OK 9899 (336)

224. CHALICE (POTIR), 1789
Alexey Kosyrev
Moscow
Silver, gilt, enamel, glass, carving,
chasing
H. 35.3, diam. 14.2
GIM 55067, OK 8493 (328)

The decoration on this chalice
demonstrates a new stylistic ten-
dency towards classicism, which
was reflected in similar objects in
the last quarter of the 18th century.

225. ALTAR CROSS, 1790
Moscow
Silver, gilt, enamel, glass, chasing
41 x 25
GIM 55071, OK 7960 (329)

226. CHALICE (POTIR), 1795
Egor Iskornikov
Moscow
Silver, enamel, gilt, casting, carving
H. 40, diam. 15.3
Illustrated on page 93
GIM 77169, OK 9859 (330)

First publication.

227. SHRINE WITH ENGRAVED IMAGES
    OF ST. ALEXANDER SVIRSKII AND THE
    CATHEDRAL OF THE INTERCESSION
    INSIDE DOORS, 1800
Moscow
Silver gilt, engraving
15.5 x 10.5 (closed)
Illustrated on page 93
GIM 103801/16 (117)

First publication.

228. CIBORIUM, 1814
Moscow
Silver, gilt, casting, chasing
H. 69.3, diam. 17
GIM 75055, OK 10063 (347)

First publication.

229. ALTAR CROSS, 1823
Michael Yakovlev
Moscow
Silver, gilt, niello, carving, chasing
39.7 x 21.3
GIM 77626, OK 10816 (344)

Acquired from the Northern
Museum of Regional Studies in
1935. First publication.

230. PURIFICATOR (POKROVETS), 1824
Moscow
Silver, silk, chasing
45.3 x 45.3
GIM 78428, OK 11147 (345)

Acquired from the Anti-Religious
Museum of Art in 1937.

CAT. NO. 226

CAT. NO. 227

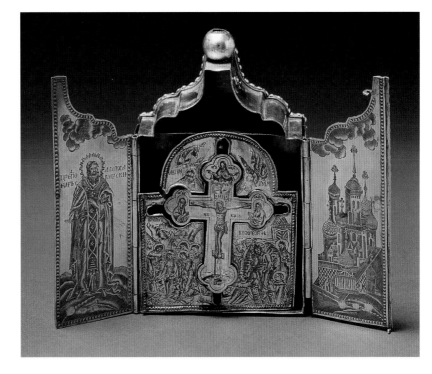

231. CHALICE (POTIR), 1829
Moscow
Silver, gilt, turquoise, paste stones,
enamel, chasing, carving
44 x 16 x 24
Illustrated on page 94
GIM 60091, OK 5660 (343)

On the bowl of the chalice are four
enameled medallions which depict
various religious figures and scenes
from the life of Jesus Christ. First
publication.

232. CIBORIUM, 1843
Fedor Andreevich Verkhovtsev
St. Petersburg
Silver, carving, casting
40.5 x 34.7 x 34.7
Illustrated on page 95
GIM 80586, OK 15216 (351)

Acquired from the State Depository of Valuables in 1940. First
publication.

233. VOTIVE LAMP (KANDILO), 1844
St. Petersburg
Silver, casting, chasing
Lamp: h. 32, chain: l. 92
GIM 68257/670, OK 9477 (340)

First publication.

234. ALTAR CROSS, 1854
Sazikov Company, Moscow
Silver, gilt, casting, carving
42 x 22
GIM 55113, OK 4193 (352)

On the front of the cross is a
depiction of the Crucifixion
with mourners, which includes
St. Tatiana, a patroness of the
Moscow University. On the back,
the inscription reads that it was
donated to the Moscow University
Church of St. Tatiana on the occasion of its centenary by graduates
of the University from Vladimir
Province. First publication.

235. SHRINE FOR RELICS, 1857
Goubkin Company, Moscow
Silver, gilt, chasing, casting,
carving
27 x 52.4 x 26.3
GIM 77239, OK 10500 (346)

Acquired from the Anti-Religious
Museum of Art in 1935. First
publication.

**236. VOTIVE LAMP (LAMPADA) ON
A CHAIN,** 1870
St. Petersburg
Silver, casting
16 x 17.7 x 17.7
GIM 53030/471, OK 4200 (339)

First publication.

**237. LITURGICAL OBJECT (PANAGIA)
WITH THE SAVIOR,** last quarter
of the 19th century
Andrey Stepanovich Bragin
St. Petersburg
Silver, amethysts, topazes, paste
stones, casing, casting, filigree
Panagia: 15.8 x 8.2, chain: l. 137
GIM 98360/31, OK 15733 (350)

Acquired from the State Depository of Valuables in 1963. First
publication.

CAT. NO. 232

CAT. NO. 238

238. WEDDING CROWN, 1899-1908
Vasily Sergeevich Sikachev
Moscow
Silver, gilt, enamel, cloth, casting, chasing
19.7 x 17.9
Illustrated on page 96
GIM 80585/2, OK 13185 (355)

Acquired from the State Depository of Valuables in 1940.

239. PERSONAL CROSS WITH CHAIN,
late 19th-early 20th century
August Hollming and Fedor Rückert, workmasters of the firm of Fabergé, St. Petersburg
Gold, enamel, precious stones
Cross: 4.1 x 5.6, chain: l. 35.5
Illustrated on page 40
GIM 68257/43, OK 6946 (358)

240. ALTAR CROSS, 1904
Vasily Sergeevich Sikachev
Moscow
Silver, enamel, paste stones, filigree
52 x 28.8
GIM 98360/49, OK 15761 (356)

241. PRIEST'S CROSS, 1908-16
Nemirov-Kolodkin Company, Moscow
Gold
H. 13.8
GIM 108076/27, OK 23487 (353)

On the order of Emperor Paul I (1796-1801), such crosses, mostly in silver but sometimes in gold, were bestowed after the occasion of the proclamation that allowed clergymen to wear crosses outside their vestments. First publication.

242. VOTIVE LAMP (LAMPADA) ON
A CHAIN, early 20th century
V. I. Flink
Moscow
Silver, casting, carving
12 x 10.8 x 10.8
GIM 101276/1550, OK 17129 (338)

Acquired from the State Depository of Valuables in 1969. First publication.

243. TAPESTRY WITH THE ASSUMPTION OF THE MOTHER OF GOD, mid-16th century
Russia
Silk (Italian), embroidery with silk, gold and silver spun thread
70 x 100
GIM 53116 RB-86 (220)

The background and border of this tapestry are patterned silk. The faces, hands, and heavenly sphere are embroidered with colored silk. Clothing, halos, wings, and architectural details are in gold and silver spun threads and colored silk.

Acquired from the collection of A. S. Uvarov in 1922.

244. SHROUD (PLASHCHANITSA) WITH THE ENTOMBMENT, 1558
Possibly Moscow
Silk taffeta, embroidery with silk, spun silver, gilt, and linen threads
67 x 65
Illustrated on page 97
GIM 54633, RB-196 (221)

In the upper part of the shroud there is a donation inscription with the names of the Grand Duke Ivan Vasilievich, the Tsaritsa Anastasia Romanovna, the Tsars Ivan and Fedor, the Tsarina Evdokiia, and the Archbishop Pimen. The date is given as 7066 (1558).

245. ICON DRAPERY (PODEA OR PELENA) WITH THE APOSTLE PHILIP, 1590-94
Moscow
Silk damask (Italian), embroidery with silk, spun gilt and silver threads
64 x 62.5
Illustrated on page 42
GIM 75371, PB-2601 (222)

A portion of the donation inscription is preserved, worked in green silk threads. It reads, "donated by Dmitrei. . . . " Because of its similarity to the podea of Demetrios of Thessalonike from the Moscow Kremlin, executed at the workshop of Dimitry Godunov's wife Matrëna, this icon drapery is dated 1590-94.

246. ICON DRAPERY (PODEA OR PELENA) WITH THE MOTHER OF GOD OF GREBNEV, second half of the 16th-first half of the 17th century
Silk taffeta, gilt satin (Turkish), embroidery with twisted silk and gilt threads
43 x 36
Illustrated on page 43
GIM 53116, RB-112 (223)

This icon drapery was donated by the nun Maria to the Church of Reverend Elijah(?). The name of Prince Cyril Andreev is mentioned in the text. The donation inscription is worked in twisted silk and gilt threads.

Acquired in 1922.

CAT. NO. 244

247. **Icon Drapery (Podea or Pelena)** **with the Annunciation,**
late 16th-early 17th century
Moscow
Silk satin, damask, twisted silk,
embroidered with silk, gilt thread
78 x 57
Illustrated on page 98
GIM 54722, RB-121 (224)

Acquired from the Rumiantsev
Museum in 1923.

248. **Altar Cloth (Aer, Vozdukh) with** **the Mother of God of the Sign,**
1606
Russia
53 x 53
Illustrated on page 42
GIM 15655 shch, RB 39, ZV 1203 (226)

Donated by Michael Saburov to
the Euphemia Monastery in Suzdal.
Acquired from the collection of
P. I. Shchukin in 1905-12.

249. **Altar Cloth (Aer, Vozdukh) with** **the Entombment,** 17th century
Russia
Silk satin (western European),
embroidered with silk, spun gilt
threads
58.5 x 75
GIM 80868/200, RB-5018 (262)

The background and border are of
silk satin. The parts of the body are
embroidered with colored silk. The
halos, clothes, wings, tomb, and
inscription are embroidered with
spun gilt threads and colored silk.
Acquired in 1941.

CAT. NO. 247
AND DETAIL

250-251. Crosses from a Liturgical Cloth (Omophorion) with the Crucifixion and the Descent from the Cross, 17th century
Russia
Silk satin, embroidery with silk, spun and filigree gilt and silver threads
25.5 x 25
GIM 15686 shch, RB-72, GIM 15687, RB-71 (240-241)

Acquired from the collection of P. I. Shchukin in 1905-12.

252. Shroud (Plashchanitsa) with Lamentation over the Dead Christ, 1625
Russia
Silk damask, embroidered with silk thread, gilt, silver spun thread, gilt thread
93 x 143
Illustrated on page 99
GIM 87844, RB-4582 (257)

According to the inscription on the shroud, Prince Dmitry Petrovich Pozharsky donated this shroud "in the year of 7133 [1625] on the 31st day of August" to the Church of the Archangel Michael.

253. Shroud (Plashchanitsa) with Christ in the Tomb, 1627
Russia
Silk damask, satin, embroidery with silk, spun gilt, filigree gilt, and gold threads
71 x 83
GIM 54433, RB-197 (225)

Donated by Ivan Shuisky to the Cathedral of the Nativity of the Mother of God in Suzdal.

254. Liturgical Vessel Cloth (Sudar), with the Mother of God of the Sign, 1627
Russia
Silk damask, ribbed silk, embroidery with silk, spun gilt and silver threads
52 x 56
GIM 54633, RB-198 (227)

Acquired from the Rumiantsev Museum in 1923.

255. Purificator (Pokrovets) with the Agnus Dei, 1627
Russia
Silk damask (Italian), embroidered silk thread, spun gilt, silver, and filigree, with ribbed silk border
52 x 56
GIM 54633, RB-199 (228)

The inscription "1C XC" was added to the purificator at a later date.
    Acquired from the Rumiantsev Museum in 1923.

256. Priest's Cloth (Palitsa) with the Descent into Hell (Anastasis), 1638
Silk, embroidery with silk, spun gilt, silver, filigree gilt threads
32.5 x 36
Illustrated on page 99
GIM 15701 shch, RB-68 (229)

Donated by the deacon Vasily Ivanovich Volkov to the Boris and Gleb Monastery of Torzhok.
    Acquired from the collection of P. I. Shchukin in 1905-12.

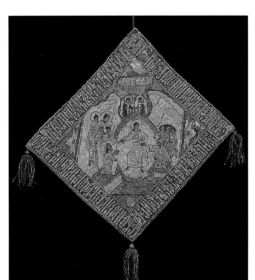

Cat. no. 252

Cat. no. 256

Cat. no. 257

Cat. no. 258

**257. Icon Drapery (Podea or Pelena)
with the Old Testament Trinity,**
early 17th century
Silk damask (Italian), silk satin
(western European), embroidered
with silk, spun gilt and silver
threads
81 x 143
Illustrated on page 100
GIM 15509 shch, RB 27 (252)

The faces, lamb, and tree are
embroidered in colored silk. Halos,
wings, clothes of the angels and
Abraham and Sarah are embroidered with gilt and silver threads.

Acquired from the collection
of P. I. Shchukin in 1905-12.

**258. Icon Drapery (Podea or Pelena)
with the Vladimir Mother of
God,** first half of the 17th century
Velvet, embroidery with silk, gilt
and silver spun threads, turquoise,
mother of pearl, and red glass
beads
66.5 x 58
Illustrated on page 100
GIM 18448, RB-34 (261)

The velvet background was put
down during the most recent
restoration. The patterned fabric
border is from the 18th century.

**259. Icon Drapery (Podea or Pelena)
with the Assumption of the
Mother of God,** 1650s
Silk satin, silk damask, embroidery
with silk, spun and filigree gilt and
silver threads
71 x 70
GIM 61491, RB-1974 (253)

**260. Thigh Shield (Palitsa or
Epigonation) with the
Crucifixion,** 1650s
Silk satin (western European),
embroidered with silk, gilt, silver
spun thread, gilt thread, tassels with
vorvorkas.
42 x 43.5
GIM 15729 shch, RB-55 (234)

A rectangle of embroidered fabric,
called a thigh shield (palitsa), was
fastened at the waist of members
of the higher clergy of the Russian
Orthodox Church.

Acquired from the collection
of P. I. Shchukin in 1905-12.

261. PURIFICATOR (POKROVETS) WITH THE AGNUS DEI, 1655
Moscow
Satin, silver thread, silk, pearls, embroidery
48 x 48.5
Illustrated on page 101
GIM 103804, NDM 3636/595, ZV-127 (75)

Donated by the Golitsin Princes to the Novodevichy Convent in Moscow.

262. PURIFICATOR (POKROVETS) WITH THE ENTOMBMENT, 1655
Moscow
Satin, silver thread, silk, pearls, embroidery
59 x 79
Illustrated on page 101
GIM 103804, NDM 5625/596, ZV-170 (76)

Donated by the Golitsin Princes to the Novodevichy Convent in Moscow.

263. PURIFICATOR (POKROVETS) WITH THE MOTHER OF GOD OF THE SIGN, 1655
Moscow
Satin, silver thread, silk, pearls, embroidery
48 x 48.5
GIM 103804, NDM 5624/597, ZV-169 (77)

Donated by the Golitsin Princes to the Novodevichy Convent in Moscow.

264. ICON DRAPERY (PODEA OR PELENA) WITH THE KAZAN MOTHER OF GOD, mid-17th century
Silk satin, embroidery with silk, spun gilt and silver threads, river pearls
38.5 x 34
Illustrated on page 43
GIM 37534, RB-33 (236)

Acquired from a private collection in 1899.

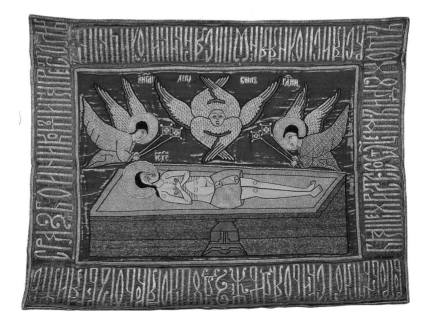

CAT. NO. 261

CAT. NO. 262

101

265. Purificator (Pokrovets) with the Mother of God of the Sign, mid-17th century
Silk damask (Italian), patterned silk (Chinese), silk (western European), embroidered with silk, spun gilt and silver threads
53 x 53
GIM 15690 shch, RB-75 (239)

Acquired from the collection of P. I. Shchukin in 1905-12.

266. Icon Drapery (Podea or Pelena) with the Deesis, mid-17th century
Satin and gilt satin (western European), embroidery with silk, spun gilt and silver threads
48 x 60
Illustrated on page 102
GIM 15975 shch, RB-26 (243)

Acquired from the collection of P. I. Shchukin in 1905-12.

267. Shroud with the Descent into Hell (Anastasis), second half of the 17th century
Russia
Damask, silver thread, silk, embroidery
48 x 50
Illustrated on page 102
GIM 103804, NDM 3833/385 (72)

From the Novodevichy Convent in Moscow.

268. Icon Drapery (Podea or Pelena) with the Baptism of Christ, second half of the 17th century
Russia
Damask, silver thread, silk, embroidery
47 x 51
GIM 103804, NDM 5618/384 (73)

From the Novodevichy Convent in Moscow. First publication.

CAT. NO. 266

CAT. NO. 267

269. Icon Drapery (Podea or Pelena) with the Mother of God of the Sign, second half of the 17th century
Russia
Damask, silver thread, silk, embroidery
43 x 45
Illustrated on page 103
GIM 103804, NDM 3818/631 (74)

From the Monastery of the Mother of God of the Sign in Moscow. First publication.

270. Icon Drapery (Podea or Pelena) with the Crucifixion with Mourners, second half of the 17th century
Russia
Silk satin, embroidery with silk, spun gilt and silver threads
67 x 59 cm.
GIM 78142/287, RB-3775 (235)

271. Icon Drapery (Podea or Pelena) with the Savior, second half of the 17th century
Silk satin, embroidery with silk and spun gilt threads
27.5 x 23.5
Illustrated on page 103
GIM 54097 shch, RB-19 (237)

Acquired from the collection of P. I. Shchukin in 1905-12.

272. Icon Drapery (Podea or Pelena) with St. Nicholas the Miracle Worker, second half of the 17th century
Russia
Silk damask, embroidery with silk, spun gilt, and silver threads
51 x 44
GIM 53116, RB-114 (260)

Acquired from the collection of A. S. Uvarov in 1922.

Cat. no. 269

Cat. no. 271

CAT. NO. 273

273. **PURIFICATOR (POKROVETS) WITH
THE AGNUS DEI,** second half of
the 17th century
Silk satin (western European),
embroidery with silk, spun gilt
and silver threads
30.5 x 39
Illustrated on page 104
GIM 15694 shch, RB-21 (238)

Acquired from the collection
of P. I. Shchukin in 1905-12.

274. **CIRCLE FROM A LITURGICAL CLOTH
(OMOPHORION) WITH THE SAVIOR
ENTHRONED IN GLORY,** second half
of the 17th century
Silk satin, embroidery with silk
and spun gilt threads
18 x 17
GIM 15689 shch, RB-74 (242)

Acquired from the collection
of P. I. Shchukin in 1905-12.

275. **PURIFICATOR (POKROVETS) WITH
THE LAMB ON THE DISCOS,** second
half of the 17th century
Satin silk, embroidery with silk
and spun gilt thread
47 x 48
GIM 78142/288, RB-3776 (258)

Acquired from the Donskoy
Monastery in 1936.

276. **ICON DRAPERY (PODEA OR PELENA)
WITH THE MOTHER OF GOD
OF THE SIGN,** second half of the
17th century
Silk satin, embroidery with silk
and spun gilt and silver threads
53.5 x 40
GIM 76509, RB-2561 (259)

Acquired in 1934.

277. **PURIFICATOR (POKROVETS) WITH THE
CROSS OF GOLGOTHA,** second half
of the 17th century
Silk satin, gilt satin, embroidery
with silk and spun gilt threads
41 x 38.5
GIM 15664 shch, RB-456 (263)

Acquired from the collection of
P. I. Shchukin in 1905-12.

278. **ICON DRAPERY (PODEA OR
PELENA) WITH THE EUCHARIST,** 1682
Silk satin (western European),
embroidery with silk, spun gilt and
silver threads
48.5 x 48
GIM 19755 shch, RB-392 (230-231)

Donated by Dmitry Jakovlevich
Chertev to the cloister of St. Nicholas
and St. Methodius in the Dmitrov
Uesd on the Pesnysh.
    Acquired from the collection
of P. I. Shchukin in 1905-12.

279. **ICON DRAPERY (PODEA OR PELENA)
WITH THE EUCHARIST,** 1682
Silk satin (western European),
embroidery with silk, spun gilt
and silver threads
50 x 49.5
GIM 19756 shch, RB 393 (231)

Donated by Dmitry Jakovlevich
Chertev to the cloister of St. Nicholas
and St. Methodius in the Dmitrov
Uesd on the Pesnysh.
    Acquired from the collection
of P. I. Shchukin in 1905-12.

CAT. NO. 280

280. EMBROIDERY WITH EIGHT DEACONS,
late 17th century
Silk satin, embroidery with silk,
spun gilt and silver threads
30 x 80
Illustrated on page 105
GIM 78280, RB-2656 (244)

Acquired from the Russian
Museum in 1936.

281. CHASUBLE (PHELONION), 17th-18th
century
Brocade, velvet, silk, embroidered
with pearls, gold, silver, decorated
with precious stones
L. 131
GIM 103804, NDM 4223/742, ZV-162 (47)

From the Novodevichy Convent
in Moscow. First publication.

282. SURPLICE (STICHARION), 17th-18th
century
Russia
Brocade, velvet, silk, embroidered
with pearls
L. 135
GIM 103804, NDM 4224/743, ZV-163 (48)

From the Novodevichy Convent
in Moscow. First publication.

283. SURPLICE (STICHARION), 17th-18th
century
Russia
Velvet, silk, silver, pearls
L. 140
GIM 103804, NDM 4219/745, ZV-158 (52)

From the Novodevichy Convent
in Moscow. First publication.

284. CHASUBLE (PHELONION), 17th-18th
century
Russia
Velvet, silk, gold, silver, embroidery
with pearls and precious stones
L. 136.5
GIM 103804, NDM 3095/744, ZV-97 (53)

From the Novodevichy Convent
in Moscow. First publication.

285. CHASUBLE (PHELONION), 17th-18th
century
Russia
Brocade, velvet, silk, gilt, silver,
pearls, precious stones, embroidery
L. 146
GIM 103804, NDM 3242/392, ZV-84 (68)

From the Novodevichy Convent
in Moscow.

286. SURPLICE (STICHARION), 17th-18th
century
Russia
Brocade, velvet, silk, pearls, embroi-
dery
L. 139
GIM 103804, NDM 3241/393, ZV-83 (69)

From the Novodevichy Convent
in Moscow.

287. CHASUBLE (PHELONION), second
half of the 17th-first half of the
18th century
Brocade, velvet, silk, gold, silver,
embroidery with pearls and
precious stones
L. 142
GIM 103804, NDM 3165/394, ZV-102 (57)

From the Novodevichy Convent
in Moscow. First publication.

288. PATEN (AER), late 17th-early 18th century
Brocade, silk, silver thread, embroidery with pearls and precious stones
78 x 53
GIM 103804, NDM 3871/423 (60)

From the Novodevichy Convent in Moscow. First publication.

289. PATEN (AER), late 17th-early 18th century
Brocade, silk, silver thread, pearls, precious stones
53 x 51
GIM 103804, NDM 1334/424, ZV-63 (61)

From the Novodevichy Convent in Moscow. First publication.

290. PATEN (AER), late 17th-early 18th century
Brocade, silk, silver thread, pearls, precious stones
52.5 x 51.5
GIM 103804, NDM 3247/425, ZV-112 (62)

From the Novodevichy Convent in Moscow. First publication.

291. ICON DRAPERY (PODEA OR PELENA) WITH ST. NICHOLAS THE MIRACLE WORKER, late 17th-early 18th century
Gilt satin (Asian), appliqué, embroidery with silk, spun gilt and silver threads,
gilt lace
53.5 x 36.5
Illustrated on page 43
GIM 54679/155, RB 1739, ZV 21272 (245)

Acquired from a private collection in 1923.

292. CHASUBLE (PHELONION), 17th-19th century
Velvet, silk brocade, lace, precious stones, glass, embroidery, appliqué
L. 137
GIM 103804, NDM 4221/746, ZV-160 (49)

From the Novodevichy Convent in Moscow. First publication.

293. CHASUBLE (PHELONION), 17th-19th century
Velvet, silk brocade, lace, gold, precious stones, embroidery, appliqué
L. 136
GIM 103804, NDM 4222/747, ZV-161 (50)

From the Novodevichy Convent in Moscow. First publication.

294. SURPLICE (STICHARION), 17th-19th century
Velvet, silk brocade, lace, silver, pearls, appliqué
L. 136
GIM 103804, NDM 4220/748, ZV-159 (51)

From the Novodevichy Convent in Moscow. First publication.

295. SURPLICE (STICHARION), 17th-19th century
Velvet, lace, gold, silver, embroidery with pearls and precious stones
L. 147
GIM 103804, NDM 3238/362, ZV-82 (54)

From the Novodevichy Convent in Moscow.

296. CHASUBLE (PHELONION), 17th-19th century
Velvet, lace, gold, silver, embroidery with pearls and precious stones
L. 153
GIM 103804, NDM 3237/363, ZV-81 (55)

From the Novodevichy Convent in Moscow.

297. SHROUD WITH THE ENTOMBMENT, 1702
Satin, silk, pearls, embroidery
174 x 107
GIM 103804, NDM 3333/753, ZV-125 (71)

The inscription on the right side of this shroud reads: "In the year of 1702 in March . . . by the will of Tsar and Grand Prince of Russia Peter Alexeevich [Peter the Great] this shroud was made and given as a gift in accordance with the promise to the Upper Petrovskiy Monastery at the time of Archbishop Iosif."

298. ROBE (SACCOS), second half of the 18th century
Patterned chenille, silk, gilt and silver threads, gilt tinsel galoon, silver buttons
L. 134.5
Illustrated on page 107
GIM 75305, RB-2590 (208)

Acquired in 1933.

299. SURPLICE (STICHARION), late 18th century
Gilt satin, silk, brocade, gilt, silver, cotton threads, gilt tinsel galoon
140 x 270
GIM 85155, RB 444639 (206)

Acquired from Kashin in 1955.

300. SURPLICE (STICHARION), late 18th century
Silk damask, patterned silk, woven lace with gilt and silver threads.
L. 138 cm.
GIM 75315, RB-2493 (207)

Acquired in 1933.

301. CHASUBLE (PHELONION), late 18th century
Russia
Brocade, embroidery with spun and filigree gilt and silver threads, cotton threads, fine gilt strip, silk, chenille, gilt galoon
L. 140
GIM 78142/85, RB-3836 (218)

Acquired from the Donskoy Monastery in 1936.

302. STOLE (EPITHRACHELION), late 18th century
Russia
Embroidery with spun and filigree gilt and silver threads, cotton threads, fine gilt strip, silk, chenille, gilt galoon and fringe
36 x 142
GIM 78142/142, RB-3700 (219)

Acquired in 1936.

303. PRIEST'S STOLE (EPITRACHELION), 18th-19th century
Russia
Satin, silver thread, flat-beaten gold thread, embroidery with pearls, spangles, and beads
140 x 34.5
GIM 103804, NDM 4348/1130 (58)

From the Novodevichy Convent in Moscow. First publication.

304. PRIEST'S STOLE (EPITRACHELION), 18th-19th century
Russia
Gold cloth, silk, silver thread, flat-beaten gold threads, embroidery with pearls and beads
143 x 38
GIM 103804, NDM 3101/1131, ZV-98 (59)

From the Novodevichy Convent in Moscow. First publication.

CAT. NO. 298

CAT. NO. 305

305. CHASUBLE (PHELONION), late 18th-early 19th century
Russia
Brocade, silk, gilt, silver, and cotton threads, chenille, gilt galoon
L. 143
Illustrated on page 107
GIM 80283/139, RB-2752 (210)

Acquired in 1939.

306. CHASUBLE (PHELONION), 19th century
Russia
Brocade, velvet, silk, silver, embroidery with pearls and glass
L. 141
GIM 103804, NDM 4218/749, ZV-157 (56)

From the Novodevichy Convent in Moscow. First publication.

307. CHASUBLE (PHELONION), mid-19th century
Russia
Brocade, silk, gilt, silver, and cotton threads, chenille, gilt galoon, and embroidery
L. 144
Illustrated on page 108
GIM 80283/59, RB-2851 (209)

Acquired from the Tretyakov Gallery in 1939.

308. SURPLICE (STICHARION), second half of the 19th century
Russia
Brocade, spun and filigree gilt, silk, and cotton threads
146 x 113
GIM 95659, RB-4850 (213)

Acquired from the Architecture Museum in 1958.

309. SURPLICE (STICHARION), second half of the 19th century
Brocade, filigree and spun gilt, silver, silk, and cotton threads, gilt brocade, copper buttons
L. 148
GIM 78142/11, RB 3910, CV-9065 (214)

310. SURPLICE (STICHARION), late 19th century
Russia
Brocade, silk, gilt, silver, and cotton threads, silver galoon and embroidery, silver button
L. 157
GIM 68257, RB-2022 (211)

Acquired in 1930.

311. SURPLICE (STICHARION), late 19th century
Russia
Gilt satin, gilt, silk, and cotton threads, fine gilt strip
144 x 103
GIM 95653/26, RB-4826 (217)

312. SURPLICE (STICHARION), late 19th-early 20th century
Russia
Velvet, silver thread, spangles, bullion, glass beads, embroidery
L. 147
GIM 103804, NDM 5222/216 (63)

From the Novodevichy Convent in Moscow. First publication.

313. PRIEST'S STOLE (EPITRACHELION), late 19th-early 20th century
Russia
Velvet, silver thread, spangles, bullion, glass beads, embroidery
150 x 32.5
GIM 103804, NDM 5218/278 (64)

From the Novodevichy Convent in Moscow. First publication.

CAT. NO. 307

314. THIGH SHIELD (EPIGONATION),
late 19th-early 20th century
Russia
Velvet, silver threads, spangles,
bullion, glass beads, embroidery
75.5 x 44
GIM 103804, NDM 5219/279 (65)

From the Novodevichy Convent
in Moscow. First publication.

315. BELT, late 19th-early 20th century
Russia
Velvet, silver threads, spangles,
bullion, glass beads, embroidery
80.5 x 11
GIM 103804, NDM 5220/281 (66)

From the Novodevichy Convent
in Moscow. First publication.

316. DEACON'S STOLE (ORARION), late
19th-early 20th century
Velvet, silver threads, spangles,
bullion, glass beads, embroidery
290 x 9
GIM 103804, NDM 5223/280 (67)

From the Novodevichy Convent
in Moscow. First publication.

317. ROBE (SACCOS), early 20th
century
After a drawing by V. M. Vasnetsov
Silk, embroidery, silver threads,
silks, bullion, spangles, artificial
pearls
L. 160
Illustrated on page 22
GIM 103804, NDM 4140/56 (94)

This liturgical robe, now in the
Pokrov Church on Ordynka Street,
was made by nuns in the workshop
of the Ivanovsky Convent.

318. SURPLICE (STICHARION), early 20th
century
Brocade, spun and filigree gilt,
silk, and cotton threads
L. 147
Illustrated on page 109
GIM 79118/1, RB-3529 (212)

Acquired in 1937.

319. ROBE (SACCOS), early 20th
century
Brocade, aksamite, spun and
filigree gilt and silver threads,
silk and cotton threads, gilt fringe,
gilt silver buttons
L. 134
Illustrated on page 109
GIM 62819, RB-3141a, CV-1375 (215)

This fabric was especially manufactured for Tsar Nicholas II's
coronation ceremony in 1896.
    Acquired from Alexander
Nevsky Lavra, St. Petersburg,
in 1928.

CAT. NO. 318

CAT. NO. 319

320. CHASUBLE (PHELONION), late 19th century
Gilt velvet, silk, gilt and cotton threads, gilt galoon
L. 138
GIM 85173, RB-4657 (216)

321. SHROUD (PLASHCHANITSA), early 20th century
P. I. Olovianishnikov & Sons
Silk, silk appliqué, embroidery with silk, spun gilt and silver threads, spangles, bugles, glass beads, and mother-of-pearl
Illustrated on page 45
110 x 171 GIM 56740, RB 1919 (247)

Acquired from the collection of the P. I. Olovianishnikov & Sons, supplier to the tsars, in 1930.

322. ICON DRAPERY (PODEA OR PELENA) WITH THE SAVIOR ON THE UBRUS, early 20th century
Brocade, embroidery with silk, spun gilt threads, spangles, glass beads, bugles, mother-of-pearl, colored stones
59 x 60
Illustrated on page 110
GIM 78142/102, RB 3721 (248)

323. PURIFICATOR (POKROVETS), early 20th century
Silk, velvet, appliqué and embroidery with silk, spun and filigree gilt and silver threads, mother-of-pearl, and glass beads
50 x 75
GIM 78142/149, RB-3722 (249)

Acquired from the Donskoy Monastery in 1936.

324. PURIFICATOR (POKROVETS), early 20th century
Silk, embroidery with silk, spun and filigree gilt and silver threads, glass beads
49 x 49
Illustrated on page 44
GIM 78142/161, RB-3739 (250)

Acquired from the Donskoy Monastery in 1936.

325. PROCESSIONAL CLOTH (GONFALON) WITH ST. NICHOLAS, early 20th century
Velvet, silk taffeta appliqué, embroidery with silk, spun and filigree gilt and silver threads, bullion
137 x 37
Illustrated on page 45
GIM 78142/257, RB-3727 (251)

Acquired from the Donskoy Monastery in 1936.

326. ICON DRAPERY (PODEA OR PELENA) WITH ST. EFREM, early 20th century
Gilt satin, appliqué of velvet and brocade, embroidery with silk, spun gilt and silver threads, bullion, spangles, mother-of-pearl, glass beads
61 x 76
Illustrated on page 45
GIM 78142/209, RB-3720 (252)

Acquired from the Donskoy Monastery in 1936.

327. TAPESTRY WITH CROSS, early 20th century
Cloth
90 x 67
GIM 56740, RB-1922 (253)

328. PALL (POKROV) WITH THE CROSS OF GOLGOTHA, early 20th century
Silk, brocade appliqué, embroidery with silk, spun gilt and silver threads, bugles and glass beads
167 x 104
GIM 69924, RB-2287 (254)

Acquired through the State Fund in 1930.

CAT. NO. 322

329. ICON DRAPERY (PODEA OR PELENA) WITH THE METROPOLITAN ALEXIS, early 20th century
Silk, embroidery with spun gilt threads
27 x 22.5
Illustrated on page 111
GIM 80175, RB-3027 (255)

330. ICON DRAPERY (PODEA OR PELENA) WITH SOPHIA ON THE THRONE, early 20th century
Velvet, embroidery with silver threads, gilt and silver woven lace
110 x 92
GIM 55942, RB-2983 (256)

331. CLOTH, early 20th century
P. I. Olovianishnikov & Sons
Gilt satin, gilt, silk, and cotton threads
79 x 59
GIM 58224/286, A-37515 (264)

Acquired through the State Fund in 1926.

332. CLOTH, early 20th century
P. I. Olovianishnikov & Sons
Satin, gilt, silver, and cotton threads
57 x 128
GIM 58224/288, A 37515 (265)

Acquired through the State Fund in 1926.

333. CLOTH, early 20th century
P. I. Olovianishnikov & Sons
Satin, silk, silver, and cotton threads
58 x 72
GIM 58224/111, A-1753 121 (266)

Acquired through the State Fund in 1926.

334. CLOTH, early 20th century
P. I. Olovianishnikov & Sons
Satin, silk and cotton threads
57 x 55
GIM 58224/121, A-1753 (267)

Acquired through the State Fund in 1926.

335. CLOTH, early 20th century
P. I. Olovianishnikov & Sons
Brocade, gilt, silver, and cotton threads
57 x 74
GIM 58224/26, A-1668 (268)

Acquired through the State Fund in 1926.

336. SHROUD (PLASHCHANITSA), early 20th century
Russia
Silk, velvet, silk appliqué, embroidery with silk, spun gilt, silver, and gold threads, spangles, bugle and glass beads, gilt galoon
103 x 174
GIM 78142/67, RB 3947 (246)

Acquired from the Donskoy Monastery in 1936.

CAT. NO. 329

CAT. NO. 338

337. MITER, 1685
Workshops of the Kremlin, Moscow
Gold, silver, diamonds, rubies,
emeralds, sapphires, enamel,
cloth, casting, chasing, smithery
H. 30
Illustrated on front cover
GIM 81538, OK 13692 (298)

This miter was commissioned by
the co-Tsars Ivan V and Peter I
(Peter the Great) and their sister
Sophia. It was donated to Gedeon
Chetverinsky, the first metropolitan
of Kiev to recognize the power of
the Patriarch of All Russia over
the Ukrainian Orthodox Church.

338. MITER, 17th-19th century
Fabric, paper, silver, precious
stones, glass
H. 21.5
Illustrated on page 112
GIM 103804, NDM 3033, ZV-95 (70)

The inscription on the rim of this
miter reads: "In the year of 1692 by
the will of the worthiest co-Tsars
and Grand Princes Ioann [Ivan]
Alexeevich, Peter Alexeevich [Peter
the Great] . . . the Autocrats of All
Russia, this miter was made for the
house of the Holiest Mother of God
of the Sign in Kitay at the time of
the first Archbishop Evfimiy."

339. MITER, 17th-early 19th century
Gold, silver, precious stones,
enamel, silk, velvet, embroidery
with pearls, chasing, carving,
casting
H. 23.2
Illustrated on page 113
GIM 77319, OK 10821 (299)

This miter was decorated with
designs drawn from both religious
vestments and lay costumes of the
15th to the early 19th centuries.
The gold lacework with holy figures
is from the 17th century, while the
embroidery with pearls and precious stones belongs to the 19th
century. The enameled images,
including the Donskaya Mother of
God, which crowns the miter, are
also from the 19th century. This
miter may have belonged to Archimandrite Afanasy Petriev (1823-32)
of the Donskoy Monastery in
Moscow.

Acquired from the Anti-
Religious Museum of Art in 1935.

CAT. NO. 339

113

340. ANDRONIKOV GOSPEL, 1980 copy
Original from the early 15th
century
Paper
29.5 x 21
Illustrated on page 46
5327, n/v OR 785 (374)

341. THE ACTS OF THE APOSTLES, 1564
Moscow
Paper, leather
28 x 17.5
86794, Shap.6 (364)

**342. PSALM BOOK OF THE GODUNOV
FAMILY,** 1594
Paper, velvet
49 x 35
80269, Uvar. 564 (363)

343. THE ACTS OF THE APOSTLES, late
15th century
Paper, leather
31 x 20 cm.
80497, Chrtk. 167 (359)

**344. THE LIFE OF ZOSSIMA AND SAVVATII
OF THE SOLOVETSK MONASTERY,**
17th century
Paper
31 x 19.5
23905, Shuk. 539 (360)

**345. DOCUMENT OF THE APPOINTMENT
OF THE PATRIARCH PITIRIM,** 17th
century
Paper, 7 wax seals, taffeta
105 x 75
80370, Sin. Gram. 1298a (372)

346. MSTISLAV GOSPEL, 1985 copy
Original from the 12th century
Paper, leather
34 x 27
Illustrated on page 46
5717, n/v OR 837 (373)

347. GOSPEL WITH OKLAD, printed first
half of the 17th century
Moscow
Gold, silver, sapphires, "ruby
crust," niello, paper, leather,
velvet, chasing, carving
38.8 x 23.8 x 9.5
Illustrated on page 40
GIM 68931, OK 6160 (295)

The plaques on the front cover of
this Gospel depict the Savior in
Glory with the Mother of God, John
the Baptist, and the four Evangelists. Following in the Byzantine
tradition, the background of the
oklad imitates rich fabric. The
non-cut, semi-precious stones
and crystals or "ruby crust" were
favorite stones of the Tsars Ivan the
Terrible, his son Fedor Ivanovich,
and Boris Godunov.
   Acquired from the Museum of
the Alexandrov Province in 1930.

348. BIBLE, 1663
Moscow
Paper, leather
36.5 x 23
86794, Shap. 1007 (365)

**349. MANUSCRIPT, "THE LIFE OF
ALEXANDER SVIRSKII,"** 1672
Moscow
Velvet, wood, paper, binding with
silver plates
33 x 22
Illustrated on page 114
GIM 103796/7 (122)

First publication.

**350. PSALM BOOK OF SIMON OF
POLOTSKY,** 1680
Moscow
Paper, leather
32 x 20
GIM 103432, Mnsh. 1909 (366)

CAT. NO. 349

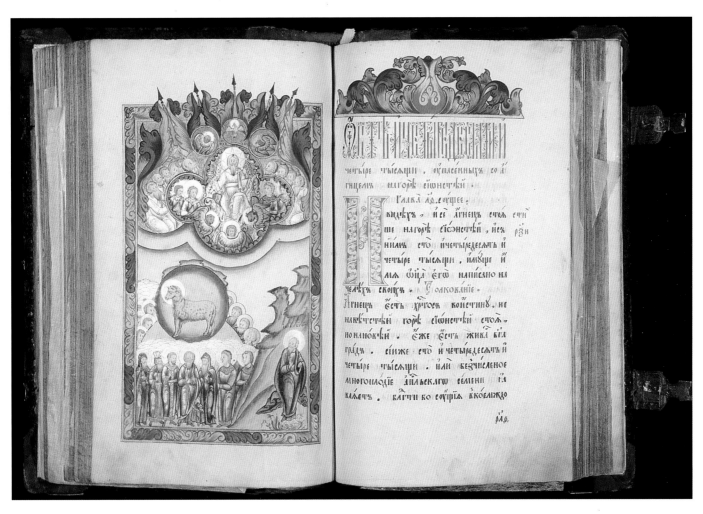

351. GOSPEL, 1692
Moscow
Wood, brocade, silver gilt, paper
40 x 30
GIM 103801/14 (112)

352. GOSPEL IN AN OKLAD, printed 1695
Oklad added 1723
Moscow
Silver, gilt, wood, paper, cloth,
casting, chasing
56.5 x 39
GIM 77299, OK 10659 (327)
In the center of the upper portion of
the oklad is the Anastasis (Descent
into Hell) presented in high relief.
On the four corner plaques is the
traditional presentation of the
Evangelists. An inscription reads
that the work was created under the
auspices of Metropolitan Joachim
of the Donskoy Monastery. The
monastery is located southwest
of Moscow on the former road to
Crimea. It was founded in 1591 by
Tsar Fedor Ivanovich to commemorate the site where the Russian military repulsed the raids on Moscow
by the Crimean Kahn Kasy-Girey.
    Acquired from the Anti-
Religious Museum of Art in 1935.

353. TITULARY, late 17th century
Paper, leather
32 x 21
82823, Muz. 4047 (362)

354. LIFE OF TSAR PETER I, 18th century
Peter Krekshin
Paper, leather
33 x 19.5
48987, Bariat. 55 (361)

355. LIVES OF THE SAINTS OF VOLOGDA,
18th century
Paper, leather
30 x 19
80269, Uvar. 107 (368)

356. GOSPEL, 1735
Moscow
Wood, velvet, silver, paper
34.5 x 23
GIM 103801/10 (113)

First publication.

357. ANTHOLOGY (SBORNIK), 1765
Paper, velvet
35 x 22
Illustrated on page 49
28822, Muz. 360 (375)

358. GOSPEL WITH OKLAD, 1772
Alexis Postnikov
Moscow
Silver, gilt, enamel, chasing,
casting, carving
73.2 x 51.2
GIM 80114, OK 12450 (348)

Acquired from the Museum of
Architecture in 1939.
    First publication.

359. LIFE OF ST. BASIL THE BLESSED,
1790
Paper, leather
23 x 16.5
28207, Muz. 32 (370)

360. LIFE OF PRINCE VLADIMIR, 19th
century
Paper, board, leather
18.5 x 11
23905, Shuk. 690 (371)

361. THE APOCALYPSE, 1859
Paper, leather
37 x 22
Illustrated on page 115
52590, Muz. 3507 (369)

362. MUSIC FOR HOLIDAYS, late 19th
century
Paper, leather
35 x 22
Illustrated on page 49
76014, Sin. Pevch. 24 (367)

363. JOURNEY TO MOSCOVIA, 1647
Adam Olearius
Schleswig
Paper, engraving
31 x 19.2
GIM 103796/795 (105)

This book is engraved with the image of the Cathedral of the Intercession (St. Basil's).

364. PORTRAIT OF TSAREVNA SOPHIA, late 17th century
Oil on canvas
93 x 82
GIM 103803, NDM 3308 (90)

From the Novodevichy Convent in Moscow.

365. NOVODEVICHY CONVENT, 1770s
Oil on canvas
130 x 95
GIM 103803, NDM 6304 (95)

From the Novodevichy Convent in Moscow.

366. PORTRAIT OF MOTHER SUPERIOR PALLADIA DUROVA, 1780s
Oil on canvas
66 x 55
GIM 103803, NDM 5838/2596 (91)

From the Novodevichy Convent in Moscow.

367. THE CATHEDRAL OF THE MOTHER OF GOD OF SMOLENSK, 19th century
Lithograph
32 x 44.5
NDM 2076 (96)

368. CHURCH OF THE ASSUMPTION, 19th century
Lithograph
29 x 40.5
NDM 2072 (97)

369. VIEW OF THE CATHEDRAL OF THE INTERCESSION AND RED SQUARE, MOSCOW. THE UNVEILING OF THE MONUMENT TO MININ AND POZHARSKY IN 1818, 20th century
Lithograph
GIM 103800/58 (106)

370. PORTRAIT OF MOTHER SUPERIOR VERA GOLOVINA, mid-19th century
Oil on canvas
34 x 32
GIM 103803, NDM 1116 (92)

From the Novodevichy Convent in Moscow.
First publication.

371. PORTRAIT OF MOTHER SUPERIOR PAISIA NUDOLSKAYA, second half of the 19th century
Oil on canvas
39 x 29
GIM 103803, NDM 1380 (93)

From the Novodevichy Convent in Moscow.
First publication.

372. MODEL OF THE CATHEDRAL OF THE INTERCESSION, early 20th century
Moscow
Papier maché
60 x 70 x 70
Illustrated on page 24
GIM VF 5108/52 (107)

First publication.

373. INTERIOR OF THE CATHEDRAL OF THE INTERCESSION (BEFORE RESTORATION), 1959
N. Baulina
Moscow
Watercolor on paper
25.5 x 52
GIM VF (109)

First publication.

374. DESIGN FOR THE RESTORATION OF THE INTERIOR OF THE CATHEDRAL OF THE INTERCESSION (COMPLETED), 1959
N. Baulina
Moscow
Watercolor on paper
25.5 x 55.5
GIM NV 6096/2 (110)

First publication.

375. HAIR SHIRT (VLASIANITSA), 1960 replica
Moscow
Cloth
138 x 50
GIM NV 4534, NV TK 306 (376)

This is a replica of a garment belonging to Tsar Ivan IV (Ivan the Terrible) in the 16th century.

376. PORTRAIT OF IVAN IV (IVAN THE TERRIBLE), 1960 copy
36 x 32
GIM IZO NV 1 (377)

This work is a copy of a painting by an unknown Russian artist. The original portrait of Ivan the Terrible was a posthumous painting made in the 17th century. It hung in Ivan's tomb in the Cathedral of the Archangel in the Moscow Kremlin, and now hangs in the National Museum of Denmark.

377. MODEL OF NOVODEVICHY CONVENT, 1982
Wood, clay, plaster
250 x 300 x 70 (scale 1:100)
NV 3017 (89)

GLOSSARY

O. G. GORDEEVA, T. I. SIZOVA,
O. B. STRUGOVA, E. V. SHULGINA

AER (Vozdukh)
A large rectangular piece of embroidered cloth used to cover the vessels containing the sacramental bread and wine (the Eucharist), which are symbols of Christ's sacrificial death. An aer was usually placed over the purificator.

AGNUS DEI
Latin for "Lamb of God." Jesus.

BASMA
Ornamental strips of metal, usually silver or silver-gilt, nailed on the surface of an icon

BAUDEKIN
A kind of rich brocade, usually with a warp of gold thread and weft of silk, smooth or patterned, sometimes with watered silk tint.

BELY
Russian for "white."

BISHOP'S CHAIR
A chair, standing on a platform on the altar, to the east of the communion table.

BITJ (Bit')
A fine gilt or silver strip.

BOYAR
A member of the upper aristocracy in medieval Russia.

BULLION
A fringe of gold and silver thread twists.

CENSER
A covered incense burner that is swung on chains in a religious ritual. The upper part often is made to imitate the roof of the church and topped with a cross. In the lower part, there is a metal grill for smoldering pieces of coal. Incense is placed on the coal.

CHALICE (Potir)
A liturgical vessel used in celebrations of the Eucharist. It holds the wine which symbolizes the blood of Christ.

CHASUBLE (Phelonion)
A long bell-shaped vestment worn by a priest during the celebration of the Eucharist. In Russia, the front has a large piece of cloth cut away so that the vestment does not impede movement of the priest's arms.

CIBORIUM
A covered vessel that holds the Eucharist.

CROSS, PROCESSIONAL
A cross, kept on a special stand on the altar and carried during religious processions.

DEESIS
From the Greek *deisis*, "praying." An image of intercession with Christ in the center and the Mother of God and St. John the Baptist standing on either side—often with additional saints and archangels—their hands raised in prayers.

DISCOS or PATEN
A liturgical vessel symbolizing the plate used at the Last Supper, and used during the sacrament of the Eucharist in the Orthodox Church. Pieces of communion bread are arranged on the discos in a precise order according to Orthodox tradition. At the center is a piece of bread called the Lamb, symbolizing Christ, and at the sides, bread is placed as a remembrance of the Mother of God.

DORMITION
The "falling asleep" of the Mother of God at the end of her life. Known in the West as the Assumption of the Virgin.

DROBNITSA
A small metal plaque of various forms, often with chasing, carving, niello, and precious stones.

ELEOUSA
Greek for "merciful." An image of the Mother of God bending to touch her cheek to the cheek of the Child. This type of composition is known as the Mother of God of Tenderness.

ENCOLPION
Greek for "on the breast." An image worn around the neck.

EPIGONATION
Thigh shield. A lozenge-shaped piece of embroidered silk, which hangs by a band from the waist on the right hand side of a priest's vestments, reaching to the knee. It was originally a handkerchief. Now it is emblematic of a sword of justice, and it is given as a reward.

EPITRACHELION
A stole or long decorated strip of cloth worn like a scarf by officiating priests.

EUCHARIST
A sacrament and the central form of worship in Christian churches, in which bread and wine are consecrated and consumed by the faithful. For Orthodox believers, the bread and wine are transubstantiated and become the body and blood of Christ.

FILIGREE GILT
A fine gilt thread wound with silk thread.

FRESCO
A painting made on freshly spread moist plaster with pigments mixed in water.

GALOON
A decorative cord made of metal and silk threads.

GONFALON
Processional cloth.

GOSPEL COVER
Precious decorations on the binding of a Gospel with images executed in various techniques. It either completely covers the board of the binding or is made of plaques (drobnitsa) laid on fabric. The central plaque of the upper plate usually depicts the Crucifixion with Mourners, but sometimes the Ressurection, the Descent into Hell (Anastasis), or the Savior in Glory are depicted. On the corners of the upper plate, there are usually images of the four Evangelists, sometimes with their symbols. The clasps often have depictions of the Apostles Peter and Paul.

HAGIOGRAPHY
Biographies of saints or venerated persons.

HODEGITRIA
Greek for "showing the way." An image of the Mother of God and the Christ Child, in which she gestures toward the Child with her right hand, indicating that He is the way to salvation.

ICON LAMP
An oil-burning vessel, suspended before icons.

ICON
Greek for "image." A depiction of sacred people or events in paintings on panel, carved wood, and other media.

ICONOCLAST
Greek for "destroyer of images." One who opposes the veneration of images, especially during the Iconoclastic Controversy of the 8th-9th centuries.

ICONOSTASIS

A screen, arranged in tiers, that separates the sanctuary of a church from the nave. It is sometimes arranged in as many as five tiers. The upper two tiers contain icons associated with the birth of Christ, the Mother of God, the Trinity, and the Old Testament Prophets. The lower tiers contain icons of the Apostles, saints, and important figures of the New Testament. The lowest level is the Local tier which celebrates the patron saint of the church, other saints especially venerated in the area or province, and icons of Christ and the Mother of God.

ILLUMINATED MANUSCRIPT

A manuscript decorated with miniatures.

KIOT

A case for icons.

KANDILO

A church lamp in the form of a large suspended icon lamp.

KOPIE

A knife with a double-edged blade in the form of a spear used for cutting the sacramental bread.

KREMLIN

The citadel of a Russian city.

LAMPADA

A votive lamp on a chain.

LZHITSA

A spoon used in an Orthodox celebration of the Eucharist to mix wine with water. Traditionally, it was a small long handled spoon with a cross at the end of the handle.

MALY

Russian for small.

MERNAIA

A "measurement" icon. When a baby was born in medieval Russia, its measurment was taken and an icon image was made of exactly that length.

METROPOLITAN

The title bestowed on a bishop who is head of a church province. A metropolitan ranks below a patriarch in the Eastern Orthodox Church.

MITER

A liturgical headdress, part of the vestments of the higher clergy. Sometimes, it was made entirely of gold or silver, but usually it was a textile-covered framework. A miter was sometimes decorated with pearls, precious stones, and images, and enameled or nielloed. The miters of archbishops and metropolitans are topped with a cross.

NIELLO

A black sulfurous substance used to fill an incised design on the surface of a metal such as silver. Niello also refers to the technique of coating an incised or engraved metal surface with a black substance made of copper, sulfur, or lead.

OKLAD

A metal cover for an icon or a book. The first Russian oklads date from the eleventh or twelfth century. During some periods, oklads covered the painting of the icon almost entirely. Pearls, precious stones, and enamels were often used for decorating oklads.

OLD TESTAMENT TRINITY

A concept from the early centuries of the Russian Orthodox Church. The image shows the meal taken by the three angels at the house of Abraham and is symbolic of the Holy Trinity and the Eucharist.

OMOPHORION

A band of cloth decorated with crosses and worn about the neck by the higher clergy.

ORANS

Latin for "praying." A representation of the posture of praying in the early Christian tradition: standing with hands open, palms out, and raised to the shoulders.

ORARION

A deacon's stole that is pinned to the left shoulder. It is embroidered with the Greek word for holy.

PALITSA

A rectangular piece of stiff fabric fastened with a rod at the waist of the robes of higher clergy.

PALL (Pokrov)

A heavy rectangular piece of cloth draped over a coffin.

PANAGIA

A special vessel worn on chains by the higher clergy over their vestments. Bread honoring the Mother of God was carried in panagias. Originally, in Russia, panagias were made of wood and ivory with decorated images of the Virgin and the Old Testament Trinity. After the middle of the sixteenth century, a panagia was a miniature icon with religious scenes. They were sumptuously decorated with pearls, precious stones, and enamels. Tsars sometimes placed their portraits on the reverse of panagias which were given as gifts. Up until the time of Peter the Great, tsars also carried panagias.

PANTOCRATOR

Greek for "the great sovereign." A frontal image of Christ holding a Gospel in one hand with His other hand raised in a blessing.

PHELONION (Chasuble)

See Chasuble above.

PLASHCHANITSA (Shroud)

See Shroud below.

PODEA (Pelena)

A cloth suspended under an icon, often embroidered with images of saints or scenes from the New Testament.

POKROV

The protecting veil of the Virgin of the Intercession.

POKROVETS (Purificator)

A linen square in the form of a cross used during the liturgy. It is often embroidered.

POTIR (Chalice)

A cup for the Eucharistic wine.

PURIFICATOR (Pokrovets)

A linen square, often embroidered, in the form of a cross, used during the liturgy.

PYX

A receptacle containing the reserved Sacrament used to carry the Eucharist to the sick.

RHIPIDION

A ceremonial fan that was carried during the liturgy to symbolize wings of angels. Usually the obverse of the rhipidion represents an image of a six-winged seraph. Rhipidions are carried only when the service is conducted by the higher clergy.

ROYAL DOORS
The central doors in an iconostasis. These doors are sometimes called holy doors.

SACCOS (Sakkos)
A robe worn first by emperors and later by patriarchs and the senior clergy. The right to wear a saccos was conferred only on patriarchs and the higher clergy as a sign of honor.

SHRINE
A receptacle in which sacred relics of the Orthodox Church were deposited. It was usually a small chest decorated with the image of the saint whose relics were kept inside.

SHROUD (Good Friday shroud)
A cloth decorated with an embroidered or painted scene of the Entombment or Lamentation of Christ. Traditionally, the shroud was taken out of the sanctuary on Good Friday.

SKLADEN
A portable folding icon, with a central panel flanked by two or more side panels. Skladens often have oklads, and may be of various sizes.

SPUN GILT
A silk or linen thread, wound with gilt thread.

STICHARION (Surplice)
A loose-fitting gown with wide sleeves worn by priests.

STOLE (Epitrachelion)
See Epitrachelion above.

SUDAR
A large rectangular piece of cloth, often embroidered, used to cover the vessels that hold the Eucharist (the paten and chalice).

SURPLICE (Sticharion)
See Sticharion above.

TABERNACLE
Holy gifts used in the celebration of the Eucharist are kept in the tabernacle. A portable tabernacle is carried on the breast of the priest in a silk or velvet container during his visit to the sick. Traditionally there was a depiction of the Crucifixion or the Last Supper on the upper cover of the tabernacle.

TEL'NIC
A pectoral cross worn by members of the Russian Orthodox Church.

TSAR
From the Latin word Caesar. In Russian, the word was first used to refer to the Byzantine emperors. Ivan IV (Ivan the Terrible) was the first Russian grand duke to crown himself tsar. Peter the Great favored the title of emperor and discarded the title tsar.

TSARITSA
The wife of a tsar.

TSAREVNA
The sister or daughter of a tsar.

TSAREVICH
The male heir of a tsar.

VESPERS DISH
A vessel used to place bread, wheat, and oil for anointing during the most solemn and long church services on the eves of important Orthodox feasts. The use of the vespers dish was connected with an ancient custom of blessing and offering "vespers bread" and wine to worshippers for refreshment during the breaks between services.

WEDDING CROWN
A crown used during a Russian Orthodox wedding ceremony. On the bride's crown there was an image of the Mother of God; on the bridegroom's, one of the Savior. During the wedding ceremony, wedding crowns were held above the heads of the bride and groom.

ZVEZDITSA (Asteriskos)
Russian for "star." A church plate, it was constructed from two metal bands shaped as a half circle, and connected with a pivot in the middle. When open, they form a cross. The zvezditsa is placed on the discos. It protects the sacramental bread when the aer is placed over it.

INDEX OF HISTORICAL NAMES

A. V. LAVRENTIEV

ST. ALEXANDER OF SVIR (1448-1533)
Canonized in 1641. Founder of one of the largest monasteries in the Russian North.

ALEXIS MIKHAILOVICH (1629-1676)
Second tsar in the Romanov dynasty. Crowned in 1645. Father of the tsars Fedor Alexeevich, Ivan V Alexeevich, and Peter I Alexeevich, known as Peter the Great. Known for piety and regular donations to churches and monasteries.

BASIL THE BLESSED OF MOSCOW (d. 1552)
Ascetic venerated even in his lifetime. Ivan the Terrible stood in awe before him. Beatified in 1544. Buried near the Cathedral of the Intercession on Red Square, also known as St. Basil's.

ULIANA DIMITRIEVNA (of the Paletsky family, d. 1574)
Consort of Prince Yuri, brother of Ivan the Terrible. Took the veil in the Novodevichy Convent after her husband's death in 1564.

ELIZABETH PETROVNA (1709-1761)
Daughter of Peter the Great. Empress 1741-62. Important advances in Russian culture, economy, and foreign policy made during her reign.

EVDOKIIA ALEXEEVNA (1650-1712)
Daughter of Tsar Alexis Mikhailovich.

BORIS GODUNOV (ca. 1552-1605)
Boyar of an old noble family descended from Golden Horde defectors. Brother-in-law of Tsar Fedor Ivanovich. Crowned in 1598. A great patron of the arts.

DIMITRY GODUNOV (d. 1605)
Boyar. Uncle of Boris Godunov. Connoisseur and patron of the arts.

VASILY GOLITSYN (1643-1714)
Boyar, Privy Councilor, diplomat, and military leader. Favorite of Tsarevna Sophia, Regent of Russia. Died near Archangelsk, where he was banished by Peter the Great after Sophia's aborted coup.

FEDOR ALEXEEVICH (1661-1682)
Third in the Romanov dynasty, and tsar since 1676. Peter the Great's eldest brother.

FEDOR IVANOVICH (1557-1598)
Tsar since 1584. Son of Ivan the Terrible and the last of the dynasty of Rurik.

FEODOSIA ALEXEEVNA (1662-1713)
Daughter of Tsar Alexis Mikhailovich.

IVAN IV, also known as Ivan the Terrible (1530-1584)
Crowned in 1533. Proclaimed himself the first tsar of Russia
in 1547. Pursued an aggressive policy of land expansion. Had the
Cathedral of the Intercession (St. Basil's) built.

IVAN V ALEXEEVICH (1666-1696)
Shared the throne with his younger brother Peter the Great,
1682-96.

BOGDAN KHITROVO (d. 1680)
Boyar in charge of the Armory Chamber in the Moscow Kremlin.
Patron of the arts.

MACARIUS (1482-1563)
Appointed metropolitan of Moscow and all Russia in 1542.
Among the government leaders in the early years of the reign of
Ivan the Terrible. Writer.

MICHAEL FEDOROVICH (1596-1645)
Founder of the Romanov dynasty. Became tsar in 1613.

MININ KUZMA (d. 1616)
Merchant. Mayor of Nizhni Novgorod. One of the leaders of the
national liberation drive in 1611-12.

NIKON (1605-1681)
Patriarch of Moscow and All Russia. Intellectual reformer of the
Russian Orthodox Church.

PAISA (of the Nudolsky family)
Mother Superior of the Novodevichy Convent in the eighteenth
century.

PALLADIA (of the Durov family)
Mother Superior of the Novodevichy Convent in the eighteenth
century.

PAPHNUTIUS OF BOROVSK (1394-1477)
Monastery founder and Father Superior. Active in Russian politics
and religion during the struggle for independence from the
Golden Horde. Canonized in 1479.

PETER THE GREAT (1672-1725)
Became tsar of Russia in 1682 and emperor in 1721. Outstanding
political and military leader. Carried out crucial reforms in all
spheres of Russian life.

DIMITRY POZHARSKY (1578-1642)
Boyar and military leader. Hero of the national liberation struggle
of 1611-12, during the Time of Troubles.

ST. SERGIUS OF RADONEZH (ca. 1321-1391)
Founder and Father Superior of the Monastery of the Holy Trinity.
Reformer of monasticism, active proponent of Russian unification.

IVAN SHUISKY (d. 1635)
Boyar and brother of Tsar Vasily Shuisky (ruled 1606-10).
Last of a powerful aristocratic family.

SOPHIA ALEXEEVNA (1657-1704)
Daughter of Tsar Alexis Mikhailovich. Regent of Russia, 1682-89, before her crowned brothers Ivan V and Peter I came of age. Deposed by Peter, she took the veil as Mother Susanna in the Novodevichy Convent. Patron of the arts.

NIKITA STROGANOV (d. 1620)
Merchant and industrialist and one of Russia's richest men. Organized Cossack expeditions to colonize Siberia, 1581-84. Head of an industrial and financial empire in northern Russia. Patron of the arts.

VASILY III IVANOVICH (1479-1533)
Grand Duke of Muscovy from 1505. Completed the unification of Russian lands around Moscow. Father of Ivan the Terrible. Founder of the Novodevichy Convent in 1524.

VERA (of the Golovin family, 19th century)
Mother Superior of the Novodevichy Convent in the mid-nineteenth century.

VASILY VOLKOV (d. after 1639)
Head of several government offices during the reign of Michael Fedorovich Romanov.